A Lonely Wonderful Walk:

A Journey of Survival and Rebirth through Cancer

by Kyle Roderick

Copyright © 2002 Kyle Roderick
All Rights Reserved
ISBN-13:
978-1530256174
ISBN-10:
1530256178

No part of this work may be reproduced or transmitted in any form or by any means, electronic or mechanical, including photocopying, recording, or by any other information storage and retrieval system, without written permission from the author.

While truth is subjective, I hope to remain honest throughout this book. Some names have been changed. Dialogue is presented as clearly as I can recall it. In some instances my mother's memory and hospital documents supplement my own recollection.

Foreword

The story I'm about to share with you is true and was written by a young man trying to find a way to process his emotions and pull meaning from a terrible experience. If you're a cancer survivor, perhaps these words will validate some of your feelings of loss, anger, frustration and confusion. Maybe it will give you an idea of how someone else has found ways to cope with this tragedy. This story may lend words to express yourself to those many loved ones who simply want to help in any way they can. At a minimum, I hope it provides you with a distraction from cancer's potentially painful world and offer a new sense of hope.

If you love a cancer survivor, this story will give you a brief glimpse of how they are feeling. Maybe it will give you an idea of how you can best help. This story may provide a foundation for mutual understanding between the person with the disease and their loved ones. It should provide you with an encouraging story of a journey through despair to a life renewed.

This journey will be painful and inspirational, anxiety-ridden yet eternally hopeful. At some point we all must face an obstacle we feel is insurmountable. It's at this point that we discover what's truly inside us. I hope that my story empowers you with the same courage it took to live through it myself.

Chapter 1

Did you think much about death before you got sick, I asked.

"No." Morrie smiled. "I was like everyone else. I once told a friend of mine, in a moment of exuberance, 'I'm gonna be the healthiest old man you ever met!'"

How old were you?

"In my sixties."

So you were optimistic.

"Why not? Like I said, no one really believes they're going to die."

But everyone knows someone who has died, I said. Why is it so hard to think about dying?

"Because," Morrie continued, "most of us all walk around as if we're sleepwalking. We really don't experience the world fully, because we're half- asleep, doing things we automatically think we have to do."

And facing death changes all that?

"Oh, yes. You strip away all that stuff and you focus on the essentials. When you realize you are going to die, you see everything much differently." He sighed. "Learn how to die, and you learn how to live."

- From "Tuesdays With Morrie", Mitch Albom

Imagine waking from a deep sleep to find yourself in a dimly lit room. A large gathering of friends gather round. You can sense they are uneasy. A young man slouches against the wall picking at a hangnail. The eyes of an older woman glisten as she peers longingly at your face - your favorite aunt. As you look up, you take note of an embarrassing drip leaving her nose. Single file they shuffle up to you. In the corner, your father embraces your mother, comforting her as she sobs quietly, but inconsolably. Her crying draws tears from the others around you. Wondering what your family and friends are doing, you mean to stand and ask them. Ineffectually you attempt to sit up. Your best friend from high school walks over slowly and you ask him for a bit of help. Instead, he kneels in front of you and water streams from his eyes, down his freshly shaven cheeks. As he grasps your hand he mumbles, "I just wish we could grab one more rum and coke, buddy." His voice quivers uneasily. "What in the hell is going on here?" You shout – but no one hears you.

Surveying the room it becomes painfully obvious. Flower arrangements line the walls. Baby blue satin pillows embrace your limp limbs. You try to scream but your mouth is sewn shut. Your eyelids are glued together, but somehow you can still see. As a younger cousin stares at your face you wonder if she can sense your eyes behind their curtains.

Your second attempt to sit up is just as unsuccessful as the first and now you're embarrassingly aware that your suit has no back. You'd always wondered if that myth about the missing back was true. Your bare backside makes a strong case as you feel the satin finish cushioning your behind. In contrast, everyone else is dressed in their best church black, backs included.

Your cousin and her boyfriend depart and finally your mother and father proceed toward you.

"Mom, dad, what happened to me? Why am I dead? How did I die?" you scream in vain.

Your parents approach. The expression on your father's face is a look you've never seen before. You know his angry face, his teasing face and his proud face. That's the one you appreciate the most. But this look – you have never seen this look.

Your mother is a wreck and her slim hands tremble as she reaches for you. Her red eyes release streams of tears that have bunched her eyelashes together into short wet spikes. You yearn to scream, to jump up and hold her. "I wish you were still here with us," your father's says calmly, but in a voice the quivers in a tone you've never heard.

"I am, I AM!" you yell.

Your mother continues, "You have made our lives worth living. We loved the way you made us laugh. Remember when you put all those clothespins in your hair at the barbecue? You looked so silly but you just did it to make us laugh." Your father forces a weak smile and then his strong face melts into something else you've never seen.

"You were so loving toward us and put up with so many mistakes. We didn't know what we were doing any more than you did. Damn, I wish we hadn't scolded you so much about your messy room," she says with a small smile. "I wish we could have known all of this. We would have held you more, called your more, visited you more. I just wish we could have you back so we could hold you one more time." Your mother begins to sob and buries her face into your father's chest. He continues for her, "Kyle, you've always made us proud and we will never forget you. Never." Your mother hangs on your father's arm as he gently closes your casket.

The hospital room slowly fades into view. Was I daydreaming again? I'm not sure I can call this horror a daydream, but I know I wasn't sleeping so that's where we'll leave it. The drugs spark many dark thoughts and, this afternoon, I find myself wondering who else might be at my funeral. I start to count how many friends would show up but I quickly lose track.

I've never spoken to a soul about these horrific thoughts before. In life, some subjects go unspoken. Of all the subjects, death may be the most taboo of all. Yet, an essential component of life is the guarantee that someday we must die. It's just part of the deal. Death has come to mean as much to me as life, if that's possible. It has taught me many lessons and given me many gifts. If you'll allow me, I'd like to share a story with you in the hope that you may also learn something about the seldom-discussed place where life and death meet like the sea and sand. There is no beginning of one and end of the other – there is only the place where they meet.

    We skirt around issues of importance to discuss inconveniences of the weather and compliment each other's new shoes. Why start a book with a discussion of death you may ask. In truth, I'm not trying to explore what happens in death, as I'm no more an authority on the subject than anyone else. Instead, I'm hoping to share with you a precious secret about life.

    To see the end is just the beginning.

Chapter 2

"Sweet are the uses of adversity, which, like a toad, though ugly and venomous, wears yet a precious jewel in its head. "
- William Shakespeare (1564-1616)

Scent has the amazing ability to remind us of times and events long forgotten. Sweet smells of summer sneak under my open single glass windowpane. I sit at my college dorm room desk staring at the computer screen and the overwhelming aroma of freshly cut grass rises from the lawn outside my room. The scent reminds me of a time much earlier than now. These memories have been stored away for some time and dusting them off floods me with emotion. It's amazing how easily we can lock away painful memories, yet they remain just as vibrant and volatile as we release them.

The little red Honda lawnmower chokes on chlorophyll as it grinds to a halt in the middle of the back yard. Damn, only one more pass and I might have been done. I detach the bag from the rear of the mower and walk toward the barrel my father has set out for me. He told me not to wait until the bag was full, but I'm a teenager and this is how I operate. My hands and sneakers are stained deep green and the scent of earth would be intoxicating if it weren't for the sweat running into my eyes.

I am a normal, healthy, seventeen-year-old boy with raging hormones and awkward facial hair. I'm growing up in a small town called Wareham, Massachusetts. My parents are married and come from large families who all live in my small town. I have one younger sister named Dana and I pick on her – but not too much. My walls are covered with pictures of swimsuit models and sports heroes. I have plenty of friends but I'm still a bit unsure of myself. I do normal things like run track, flirt with girls, fight with my parents, drive, and, most importantly, I'm pretty sure I know everything. I own the world.

I was not always like this though. As a child, I was ill more often than most of my friends. The pediatrician, Dr. Conway, was both a trusted friend and mortal enemy. It was frustrating to have a constant cough or the sniffles, so I avoided telling my parents as often as I could get away with it. Then one day, in the fall of 1994, I woke up with a sore throat: Man, I'm sick again. My throat is killing me. I'm so sick of being sick, but I'm not going to the stupid doctor's office again. I'll just get some rest.

I was reluctant to inform my mother. She was always worried that I had the latest virus. Everything became an ordeal once she heard me cough or sneeze. "Oh my God, are you sick?" she'd exclaim as if it wasn't a question but rather an opportunity for her to solve a problem. It seemed exciting to her.

My mother, Betty Ann Roderick is a pale skinned white woman with red hair, green eyes, and freckles. A wonderful mixture of Irish, Scottish, Swedish and other European bloods dance the jig through her bloodstream. Her fiery red hair helps to underscore her personality. Her passion and intelligence are assets she uses wisely, albeit annoyingly to a teenage son. My mother raised me to adhere to high moral standards and constantly highlighted the importance of education. "I always got straight A's," she told me constantly and with pride. I inherited her strong-headedness and independence which led to epic battles over the lack of cleanliness of my bedroom floor. She is the stricter parent and our relationship hasn't always been smooth. Since my father works long weeks, mom was usually left to dole out the punishment.

In retrospect, I know her intentions were good. She only wanted me to grow up with clear direction and a good education. Unfortunately, teenagers do not care about direction or arithmetic, and I was no exception. As I've matured and my mother has relaxed, our relationship has finally begun to grow into one we have both longed for. With my departure to college, we learned how to lay down our defenses and our relationship seemed to blossom.

However, during these younger years, I was reticent to initiate a conversation about the golf balls growing in my neck. My adolescent brain therefore decided I should take care of things without her help. I drank gallons of orange juice and indulged in additional sleep. In retrospect, it seems foolish to think that my home remedies would stave off the battle that was unfolding.

First, the lymph nodes in my neck enlarged. They became painful to the touch and I couldn't sleep for almost three full days and nights. I finally had to confess to my mother. It seemed like we were at Dr. Conway's office within minutes. "I'm not sure what he has, Mrs. Roderick," he told my mom. "I think we should send his blood to the lab. He could have mono." After testing my blood for multiple antigens, the results came back negative, including mono. Dr. Conway then wrote a prescription for an antibiotic and Tylenol with codeine every four hours. Medicine never has been an exact science and this case was no exception.

Over the following two days, my lymph nodes continued to swell and were impressively tender. I took the Tylenol every four hours, and Ibuprofen in between. As the lymph nodes grew, my breathing became more labored. My mother was frantic and demanded another immediate appointment with the doctor. Dr. Conway was concerned about the ineffectiveness of the antibiotic and admitted me to the local hospital for observation. Luckily my mother worked at Tobey Hospital so she was able to keep a close eye on me. It seemed like she came up to my room almost hourly. "Are you alright? Are you feeling any better? Do you need anything?" She'd ask in rapid succession before I could answer. "I'm fine," I'd reply weakly.

Unfortunately, I continued to deteriorate and was in massive pain. My head pounded and I lost the ability to swallow solid foods. In addition, my best friend, Erik, had come down with a similar condition and his physician also admitted him to Tobey. Whatever we had, we had a bad case of it. We were exhausted, weak, feverish and in pain.

Erik and I had been crashing our big wheels into things since before kindergarten. We were practically inseparable. We rode our scooters off the sand dunes at the end of the street to see which one flew higher (actually, it was my sister's scooter). We constructed impenetrable fortresses for our G.I. Joe action figures in the sandbox. I was even with Erik when I first got in trouble for using the "F" word. The neighbor's dog, a stupid, mopey beagle that we were convinced wanted to maul us, chased us down the street where I conveniently ran into my mother as I uttered the profanity of all profanities. Yep, Erik was there through it all.

He and I were now facing a difficult illness together. Fortunately for Erik, he made a miraculous recovery and was discharged from the hospital after four days. I was cheered to hear my buddy had recovered so quickly. However, my journey was just beginning. After the better part of a week, Dr. Conway decided it was time to transfer me to a more sophisticated institution. My lymph nodes had continued to swell and were starting to compromise my airway. I gasped for breath and my fever ran above 104. Everything seemed to be deteriorating.

"Mr. and Mrs. Roderick, we've done all we can for Kyle here. It's time to send him to Boston before this progresses any further," He declared. Boston? Why can't they just figure it out here? The ambulance parked outside the Tobey Hospital emergency department and I was terrified. They were transporting me to the renowned Children's Hospital in Boston. I still remember exactly what Doctor Conway said to me as the gurney wheeled out of my hospital room toward the back door. My mother and father walked despondently beside me, as I pleaded to anyone that could hear, "I don't want to go, please don't make me leave!" Doctor Conway turned to me with a smile on his face.

"Kyle, the worst thing they're going to do is cut your neck open," he said, crossing his teeth in a horribly distasteful attempt at humor.

"Cut my neck open? Cut my NECK open? What is he talking about?" I gasped to my mother in astonishment. "I don't want to go. Just leave me here, I'm sure I'll be fine!" To this day, I doubt my mother forgives him.

Despite my objections, my father and I were loaded into the ambulance and on our way to Children's Hospital. I remember the ride fairly well - given my grave condition. My father was allowed to ride in back to help comfort me on the ride to Boston. Dad never did say much, but he was always there. He is a man who works too much and balances humor with life lessons.

My father, Michael Roderick, is a Cape-Verdean American, middle-class, athletic man. Cape-Verde is a group of islands off of the western coast of Africa. Provinces of Portugal during the times of colonialism, the islands were used as a stopping point for slave ships on their passage across the Atlantic to the New World. The extensive interracial mixing on the island produced a people with an incredibly diverse set of features that positions them in their own ethnic category. My father looks like a lighter-skinned black man, with African hair, but a "noble" (as opposed to a "broad" nose). He is a handsome man who has been my lifelong hero.

My father teaches me many lessons that continue to improve my life. He has taught me the value of hard work, planning, respect and courtesy. He has always been an admired and popular man in our community. At times, his hard work philosophy has been overbearing, but as a man who never works less than six days a week, I see where he must be coming from. He works as a construction inspector during the week and is a self-employed landscaper on the weekends. He's shown me how to talk to people with respect and to approach conflict with my mouth rather than my fists. Dad has also taught me the value of laughing at oneself, of trying new things, and that actions speak volumes more than words.

    This man joined me in the back of that ambulance as the lights flashed blue and red, and the siren began to wail. "It'll be alright, Kyle," he said as he mopped my sweaty forearms with a damp, white towel. "We'll be there in no time." His voice was comforting, but not all together sure.

    I wonder now what my father must have felt as he rode in the back of an ambulance with his only son. Despite his strengths, he was ill prepared to deal with this unusual situation. Dad is the "fixer" of our family. A busted toy, fuzzy cable, leaky toilets were all repaired as soon as he could get to them. His practical advice was always timely, useful, and usually found a way to jump our generation gap and strike home. Dad always fixed things. He could usually make me laugh. This time, trapped in the back of a speeding ambulance, he could do nothing.

As my father comforted me, I stared through one of the small portholes at the top of the cabin. It's odd to be that person inside the ambulance. So many times we see and hear them driving by and think, "I wonder what happened, I wonder who's in there?" This time, I was "in there."

I watched the lights painting the trees and buildings in broad strokes of red and blue as we drove by. There was an element of excitement, akin to a child who climbs inside a fire truck for the first time. The most astonishing feature of the ride was that I could hardly hear the siren. Why is it so quiet in here? It's difficult to get closer to the siren than actually inside the ambulance, yet it didn't appear very loud to me at all. I found the muted siren strange because it was contrary to my expectations.

That small detail entertained my overheated brain as we drove an hour to the city. I had an amazingly high fever, and was sopping wet with sweat. My father continued to wipe my arms and forehead. "We'll be okay, we're almost there," he whispered as we barreled down the interstate. As my eyes rolled around in my head and breaths came more slowly, I wondered if I could be fixed before it was too late.

Chapter 3

"Man can learn nothing unless he proceeds from the known to the unknown"
                    - Claude Bernard (1813 - 1878)

We finally arrived at the Children's Hospital emergency room and were pushed off into a corner to wait until someone could take me into surgery. My father and I entered an entirely different world than the small town community hospital we'd left. In the hustle and bustle of the urban emergency room we no longer knew the nurses and their families. I felt a sudden transformation from a person, with feelings and a history, to a chart. My chart hung from the footboard of my gurney ready to pronounce my condition to the resident lucky enough to pick up my case. My father stood impotent and frustrated, as I lay motionless amid the flurry of white lab coats and beeping machines.

It was late in the evening of Friday, April 15th, 1994. After a half-hour, a resident unlocked the wheels of my gurney and we traveled up to one of the hospital floors. I was admitted with what was assumed to be an extremely severe case of mono. Well, at least that's what my chart said. "I'll be back in a few minutes," he said hurriedly. The resident grabbed the clipboard at my feet and set off to solve a problem. This was the healthcare system I was now entering.

If he was a typical resident, this poor guy was likely ending a twelve hour shift that started at

7am and could hardly see straight. He might have just finished two intense years learning biology, chemistry, pathology and anatomy. He'd spent hours in the laboratory carving into human cadavers, routinely desensitized to the soul with the skin he has had to cut. Classes on interpersonal skills and bedside manner are rare and of little importance to most of his peers. After entering the world of medicine he will swear to follow the Hippocratic Oath. In that proclamation, he will swear to, "Pay the same respect to my master in the science as I do to my parents, and share my life with him and pay all my debts to him. I will regard his sons as my brothers . . ."

From my experience, this oath has unfortunately rung hollow for some of the overworked and underpaid clinicians I've met. Many physicians have been able to preserve the love they have for humanity. Many still remember why they dedicated their lives to the service of their brothers. Unfortunately, too many have been robbed of their dedication by endless caffeinated hours memorizing pages from medical texts and writing reports for Fellows and Attendings. Still others survive this rigorous training and enter the community with a caring heart, only to be offered lower and lower payments by state and private insurance companies.

Thus introduces the complex world of the medical hierarchy. This strange phenomenon doesn't help my poor resident maintain his humility nor humanity. Every day, Attending Physicians at the hospital haze the Fellows. In turn, the Fellows take their frustration out on this resident. This cycle is designed to test his resilience and force him to quickly and accurately form a diagnosis and treatment plan. The medical profession will expect him to learn the confidence to perform his job with efficiency. An undecided physician will never earn the respect of his colleagues.

This resident is also put to work for a number of hours that frazzle his nerves and test his mental and physical endurance. Until the 1990s, hours for residents routinely surpassed seventy-five to one hundred hours per week. That is until the famous case of an eighteen year-old named Libby Zion, the daughter of a well-known New York reporter, who was admitted to Cornell Medical Center. Libby died after receiving two medications from an overworked and overtired medical resident that caused a lethal adverse reaction. In November 1999, the Institute of Medicine (IOM) of the National Academies released a report revealing that medical errors kill 98,000 patients and injure many others every year in the United States, racking up costs of $8.8 billion to our health-care system. More people die from medical mistakes each year than from highway accidents, breast cancer or AIDS.

While the work hours required has declined since the much-publicized death of Libby Zion, this barbaric system remains in place. Some argue that the system should remain due to tradition or as a rite of passage for all physicians. Arguments have also been leveled relating to the need for residents to see the evolution of disease so as to gain a better understanding. Perhaps most morally questionable, the system is needed so that hospitals can continue to operate on the cheap labor of medical school residents and remain within their operating budgets.

Finally, the American Healthcare System has become amazingly commercialized, capitalized, and economically complex. Insurers provide financial incentives to physicians to write for particular drugs, tests and to discharge patients from the hospital sooner. Pharmaceutical companies develop elaborate contracting and rebate deals with insurers and states to remain accessible to the physicians and patients covered by those insurers. Hospitals must make tough choices on which departments to sustain based on cash flow analyses. For example, while an emergency room hemorrhages money caring for uninsured walk-ins, a new cardiac wing can bring in extra money. Physicians are forced to stop accepting Medicare patients because the government does not reimburse them enough. Employers must also pass on the rising cost of health insurance to their employees in the form of higher co-payments and premiums. Insurers are constantly cutting costs, reducing the amount they reimburse physicians.

Despite the efforts to control costs, patient advocacy groups scream for the use of new diagnostic tools and treatments that are not covered. Pharmaceutical companies are trying to develop the latest treatments for cancer and

Alzheimer's disease while facing competition from generic drug makers and public backlash over the cost of prescription drugs. Then this resident, who has been working for the last eleven hours, picks up my chart. He is expected to make me well without breaking the bank. Can I blame him for being impersonal?

A cursory examination of the other side of this human interaction may explain a contradiction that lies at the heart of why so many feel disenchanted with our healthcare system. In the dictionary, the first definition of the word "patient" is, "capable of bearing affliction with calmness." The second definition is, "capable of bearing delay and waiting for the right moment." This conjures for me images of endless hours reading year-old issues of worn Reader's Digest magazines in any number of waiting rooms.

As patients, we are forced to sit calmly, whether in pain or febrile, as our physicians fill out paperwork on an ever increasing patient population. By the end of the day, patients are arriving on time for appointments only to learn that their doctor has fallen an hour behind schedule due to unforeseen calls from pharmacies, HMOs and unhappy customers. As people sit longer in waiting rooms across the country, perhaps we should begin to pronounce the word twice each time we say it – patient patients.

This group of ill-feeling people watch their insurance premiums rising steadily year after year only to see services decline. Medicines that improve the quality of their lives and keep them out of the hospital for asthma, heart disease and diabetes are becoming overpriced. They've come to feel entitled to a high level of service in every other American industry and are now forced to insist on tests, as their physicians must balance medical need with a personal financial gain to withhold services.

It was within this system that I waited in the Children's Hospital emergency room. Within an hour, the otolaryngologist (the funny longer name for the ear, nose, and throat doctor) Dr. Dwight Jones, arrived to assess the situation with my lymph nodes. He seemed knowledgeable enough to me. Although, drugged up as I was, he might as well have been the janitor. I lay gasping for air as the industrious residents set about reading through my charts and dripping intravenous antibiotics to slow the progression of whatever infections might be attacking my body.

Dr. Jones' immediate concern was the lack of oxygen getting to my lungs. The lymph nodes in my neck had swollen so massively that the airway was slowly but steadily closing shut. An oxygen saturation monitor clipped on the end of my finger showed that the oxygen levels in my blood were dangerously low. Even with an oxygen cannula in my nose, the saturations were only reading thirty percent - nowhere near the average ninety five percent. I lay panting in my bed, disoriented and scared. Lack of oxygen to my brain left me dizzy and confused. The only thing I knew was that I could breathe while I was lying on my right side. If I rolled onto my back, or stomach, or my left side, I could not draw in an ounce of air. It was time to act – quickly. My father grew palpably anxious as Dr. Jones consulted with his residents.

The team of doctors at Children's decided that they must intubate me (force a tube down my throat) to eliminate the possibility that my neck would swell shut and suffocate me. An emergency operating room was procured and I was quickly wheeled downstairs. Dr. Jones scrubbed up and began to prepare the operating room. This was not a sophisticated procedure, but my airway was drastically constricted – it would be difficult to get the plastic tubing into my throat.

After I was wheeled into the operating room, Dr. Jones explained the procedure and gave the anesthesiologist, a much older gentleman, permission to put me to sleep. The anesthesiologist was old and looked fragile. He was perhaps a few years from retirement and I was a routine procedure in his day. As the physicians spoke, I watched their lips move and only thought, I don't care what you're going to do, or how you're going to do it. I just want to breathe!

The anesthesiologist readied the gas mask for my mouth. I was lying in a fetal position on the operating table. I lay this way not only because I was scared, but also because it was the only way that I could draw a breath. The poor anesthesiologist didn't know this. He had no idea what I was thinking or feeling. He just wanted to put the seventeen-year-old male with severe lymphadenopathy to sleep. The old man began to roll me onto my back. "Okay, son, we're just going to get you ready here," he said quietly. I remember this part clearly, in stark contrast with the rest of my experience at Children's Hospital.

The man rolled me over and I immediately became rigid. I tried to speak. I tried to yell! I wanted to scream to them, "I can't breathe, I can't freaking breathe!" Didn't they know I could only breathe on my side? Didn't they know that? Crap... I got as far as "I ca..." and I had no wind left to finish the sentence. Now, this was quite a predicament. I was lying on my back with this old man holding down my shoulders and I couldn't talk. To make matters worse, the gas mask had already been placed over my mouth. My eyes grew large and shifty. I was terrified that I couldn't breathe, and this man was holding me down! As the adrenaline began to pump, I did the only thing I could to get out of the situation - I cocked back my right arm, swung with a closed fist as hard as I was able and decked the old guy right on the point of his chin. His head snapped back as he released my shoulders as he clutched his jaw. "What the hell?" he exclaimed. He looked at me, confused and a little angrily. I rolled back onto my side and gasped for air.

These professional men and women stood around astonished at what had just happened. He looks like such a nice young man, they must have thought. Finally, Dr. Jones leaned over - cautiously. "Kyle, is everything alright? What's the matter?" he ventured.

"I can… only breathe . . . on this side," I stutter.

"Okay, okay, we'll leave you this way then," he said with relief. The poor anesthesiologist then administered the gas, while I lay curled on my side, and I drifted off to sleep. Dr. Jones later said he could barely get the tube in my throat because it had swollen so severely. Luckily, they didn't have to cut my neck open.

Unfortunately, intubation only solved part of the problem. My body was still being ravaged by an unknown infection and losing. A normal white blood cell count ranges from 4,000 to 10,000. By Sunday afternoon my white cell count had risen to 35,000 and the doctors feared the massive disease was threatening my life. One of Dr. Jones' residents took my mom aside at this point and leveled with her. He spoke to my mother with well-meaning intention, "Mrs. Roderick, some kids get mono, get sick, and get better. Some kids get mono, get sick, and die." According to The Chart, things didn't look good for this kid.

Chapter 4

"The art of medicine consists in amusing the patient while nature cures the disease"
- Voltaire (1694-1778)

Dr. Jones and his team were quickly running out of options. My feverish, damp and limp body was wheeled upstairs to the Intensive Care Unit of Children's Hospital. As the infection spiraled out of control, the ICU team attached me to a respirator to control my breathing. The team of doctors increased the dose of intravenous antibiotics and continued to look for possible solutions. My mother had arrived at the hospital later the same morning and she and my father huddled at my bedside hoping and praying for improvement. Later that Sunday evening, my mother asked Dr. Jones if I might have a severe case of sepsis (an extreme blood infection). He told her that it might be possible, but no one had ordered those tests yet. They ordered the tests and continued to wait.

By Wednesday, the plastic and metal respirator had entirely taken over for my lungs. My situation was rapidly deteriorating. While the blood tests couldn't confirm it, Dr. Jones and his team's best guess was that I simply had a terrible case of mononucleosis. However, other infections had begun to set in which complicated the situation. Sepsis was likely the worst problem and was remained uncontrolled. Bronchitis, pneumonia, sinusitis, ear infections and eye infections also broke through the antibiotics – we're talking complete meltdown here. I mean, as if the situation weren't dire enough, I had a freaking ear infection.

There was massive lymphadenitis in my neck and face. In fact, during a rare period of consciousness, a medical resident asked my permission to take a picture of my impressively inflated face – I nodded my approval. Dear God, what must my parents have felt at this point? The Chart and their only son were moving across the spectrum from "hopeful" to "write the first draft of the eulogy".

I can imagine the scene between my mother and father.

"Is there anything else we can do?" my mother would say as each word grasped for hope. Her pale nose would turn red as she started to cry.

"Betty, we need to stay calm. I'm sure they're doing as much as they can," my father would reply with hollow reassurance.

"I cannot lose him. I cannot lose my son, Michael. He means the world to me."

"I know. I know."

During my stay in the ICU, few friends were allowed to visit. However, the persistent breeds were able to sneak in. I recall a vision of my friend Mary Catherine and her mother walking past the bed not recognizing a face they had known for years. They briefly looked into my curtain-cubicle and not a trace of recognition crossed their eyes. Mary Catherine would later explain that she couldn't identify the pale and swollen face she saw until she walked back and read the name on the bed. I was losing this battle and I feared that the horrible picture of my face would be published in some medical textbook along with a synopsis of my Chart. I could not let The Chart win, but I didn't even know my name at this point. In fact, I didn't even recognize my own parents. I was scared.

Given the failing state I was in, my mother had the instinctual feeling that I wasn't responding to the antibiotics the physicians were administering. While the mono was a virus, the septicemia and assorted bacterial infections should be reacting to the drugs. I should have been improving with these antibiotics and she refused to let me slip away. Mom took to attacking the helpless residents. She went into the medical resident's office late one night and screamed at the resident in charge.

"I knew he has more than just mono!" she said, nostrils flared. "Something isn't right, he is not responding to the antibiotics. What is he on? Can we culture him to see if the bacteria is resistant?"

The resident's words dripped with condescension, "Kyle is in the best children's hospital in the world and there is nothing else that we can do." He added, in a moment of disappointing insensitivity, "Mrs. Roderick, some kids get sick and they get better. Some kids get sick and die. We're doing all we can."

"I WANT you to culture him. Make sure he isn't resistant!" she screamed. Then she stormed out.

After my mother's tirade, the resident performed the culture she requested. An hour later, a smiling nurse found my mother in the lounge and announced proudly, "You were right ma'am, he has two organisms; Staph Aureus and Pseudomonas. They were resistant to clindamycin" Dr. Conway had indeed prescribed clindamycin for recurring infections over the previous year and I was receiving the IV form of clindamycin in the intensive care unit. I fear what might have happened had my advocate not been present - and loud. I guess you can be in the best place in the world, but sometimes you still need a little help from a loving mother.

The ICU team switched the antibiotics and I immediately showed signs of improvement. My white blood cell count dropped from 38,000 to 5,000 in thirty-six hours, which demonstrated a decrease in infection. The fever, which had remained close to 106 degrees, approached more normal levels. Color and life returned to my face and my mind began to focus again. Once the fever had subsided, my name came back to me and several hours later I recognized my Aunt Claire. In total, I remained in the Intensive Care Unit for twelve days; ten days on a respirator.

Shortly before transferring me back to the regular ward, Dr. Jones and his residents decided it was time for the tube to come out of my throat. We were in the hallway on our way downstairs when he seemed to decide it was time. This is a little odd to be doing in the hallway. I struggled to sit up and he told me that, like a Band-Aid, it would hurt less if they ripped it out than removing it slowly. After ten days in my swollen throat, however, the serrated white plastic tube was secured in place by inflamed and infected tissue. It took a great deal of effort for one of Dr. Jones' cronies to tear it from my esophagus. I would have screamed but searing pain in my throat made it impractical. "There, that wasn't so bad, was it?" he asked with evident sincerity.

Once back downstairs, another team of doctors walked across the street from the highly esteemed Dana-Farber Cancer Institute to examine me. The team had considered taking a bone-marrow aspirate. This procedure involved a long large bore steel needle, your pelvis and an immense amount of pain. However, the team determined that since Lymphoma cells appear similar to Epstein Barre cells (the virus that causes mono) under the microscope, the tests were likely to be inconclusive. They decided simply to wait and watch.

As I recovered in the hospital, I received a great deal of love and support from my family and friends. Get well cards and letters came every day but the most touching gift was a get well banner signed by almost everyone in the high school. They had all signed it and written short messages explaining how they missed me and wished for a speedy recovery.

I also got one short reprieve from my jail term in the hospital. Shortly after moving back to the regular ward, I got a letter that I was accepted into the National Honor Society. But the induction ceremony was only a few days away. I wasn't allowed to leave the hospital until I'd gone without a fever for forty-eight straight hours. At first, the doctors said I couldn't leave for the ceremony, but after much pleading and cajoling, they agreed to let me return home for a few hours. No one knew about this little plan except my co-conspirator; my father. My mother surely would have vetoed the idea in a heartbeat so we thought it best to keep it a secret.

We set off for the ceremony with a short stop at home to pick up my mother (who really let us have it) and my sister. We showed up at the high school where no one expected to see me. My friends and teachers were amazed to see me and got a good laugh out of my antics to weasel out of the hospital.

During the ceremony, one of the school's favorite teachers, Mr. Sylvia, made an announcement:

"Kyle Roderick made a special visit to us tonight, and I heard a rumor he told the nurses that if they didn't let him come down here, he was going to have the whole high school up to the hospital to protest in the hallways," he announced to the audience. "We're so glad to have him here."

I was glad to be around too.

Four long weeks passed before I returned home to my family, friends and real food for good. Perhaps the person most excited to see me was my sister, Dana. At this stage in our lives we were finally beginning to grow out of our fighting sibling drama and growing together toward a more loving and valued relationship.

We shared many things: parents, extended family, demeanor, sense of humor and ancestry. Dana and I are often asked, "What are you?" when people see the color of our skin. The complexion varies from a light brown in the winter to a deep healthy tan in the summer. Our facial features don't surrender much information either. I have a "noble" nose like my father and had long loose curly blonde hair when I was younger. My sister has a button nose and wavy brown hair with blonde highlights. She is stunningly attractive with a mischievous glint to her caramel eyes and the promising aura of a girl waiting to blossom.

Dana's beauty is only surpassed by her innate ability to make people around her smile when she wishes them to. She is seven years my junior and wasn't always my favorite. When Dana was born I was spiteful and resented her theft of the spotlight. As we've both grown, she changed from a pesky little sister to a beautiful young woman with a big heart and a sharp wit. She also inherited the athletic gene in the family and was an all-star in almost every sport she tried. She's endured living in the shadow of a successful older brother and still stayed out of trouble. I would do anything for my sister, and she looks up to me in a way that fills me with pride every time I think about it. As time passed, we became closer and as we got older, she became one of my best friends.

With Dana helping me to recuperate, I was back to my old self in no time. I returned to high school and everyone seemed pleased to see me. However, my biggest worry was a hormone driven desire to find a date to the junior prom, which was only two weeks away. I had been looking forward to going all year, but had been in the hospital for so long that everyone else had procured a date before I got home. Man, all the girls are already taken. Who am I going to get to go to the prom with me?

Luckily, a good friend from another school, Missy, agreed to be my date. I had quite a crush on Missy and had a wonderful time at the dance. She even humored my best friend Erik with a dance as he proceeded to imitate some dances from Michael Jackson's "Thriller" video; much to my horror. During the prom my friends dedicated the song "That's What Friends Are For" to me. Our collective wishes came true and I made it out of the hospital with no visible harm. We locked arms on the dance floor as Stevie Wonder and Diane Warwick sang sappy, but appropriate, lyrics. This scary chapter in my life was finally coming to a close. The blue and red lights were gone. The fevers and pain were gone. I was safe within this extended hug, wrapped in friendship and precious immortality yet again.

Unfortunately, this chapter of my life was not ending. It was just beginning. Locked arm in arm at that junior prom, everything seemed absolutely sublime. However, my angry body was slowly starting to destroy itself from the inside. The severe infection that hospitalized me had done serious damage to my lymphatic system and something within me was mutating and changing even as I danced at the prom. It probably started with one cell, hurt so badly during the war that it went haywire. It began to reproduce and wouldn't stop. A new path for my life was emerging inside this one tiny cell.

Chapter 5

"Never measure the height of a mountain until you have reached the top. Then you will see how low it was."

- Dag Hammarskjold

    The remainder of my junior year went by disarmingly smooth. I worked at Papa Gino's during the summer spinning pizza dough in the air and cooking steak and cheese subs. I looked forward to my senior year with much anticipation. The summer was filled with trips to the beach, walks through the mall, talks on the phone and, best of all, driving my parents up the wall. Senior year was when it was all going to happen! I'd been an involved student with great grades and I knew it would to pay off with an acceptance to the college of my choice. I returned to the social enigma that we call high school, ready to take on the world.

    Senior year began well. I was in class with all my friends and the Terrible Illness seemed a small part of my past. However, in October of my senior fall, I developed a sore throat that concerned my doctors. While I'd been in the hospital, Dr. Jones decided he should remove my tonsils during the following Christmas break. Tonsils are a common epicenter for Epstein Barre infections. Removing them might decrease the risk of a recurrence. This new sore throat gave Dr. Jones some concern I might develop another life threatening infection so made the decision to remove my tonsils immediately.

"I want you to come up next week and we'll just take them out," he stated flatly. We scheduled a surgical day at his office in Children's Hospital and drove to Boston a few days later for the operation. The tonsils were sent for biopsy and pathology tests were performed as a routine screening for anything abnormal. My mother treated me to ice cream and a few days out of school.

A few days later, we received an alarming call from Dr. Jones' secretary. "Mrs. Roderick, the pathology report came back inconclusive. They saw something they didn't like, but want to do a few more tests to get a better understanding. I'll call you as soon as we know anything." Her voice was calm, but the message troubled my mother.

I, on the other hand, took it in stride. I was blissfully oblivious to the ramifications of an alarming pathology report. I'm only seventeen years old. I'm invincible! I'm, like, totally immortal!

Having just survived a horrific bout with mono, I was recovering effortlessly from the tonsillectomy and enjoyed a few days out of school. This report meant nothing to me. As a teenager, I was positive that nothing could harm me. I never thought all the testing and phone calls would amount to anything more than a scare. It was something to pay attention to, but not to fear. At least, not yet.

However, the weeks passed and turned into a month. I wasn't sure whether I should be relieved or frightened. As three weeks turned into four, then five, then six, I become increasingly nervous. My carefree attitude was rapidly changing. What could be wrong? Why is it taking so long to figure out what's up? How can they call and say, "Something's wrong" but not know what?

My family joined in my quiet desperation for an answer. As each week passed, our anticipation grew. Dr. Jones set up a meeting for us with an oncologist at the Dana-Farber Cancer Institute. He said, "I want you to be prepared for all the possibilities. The specimens are going all over the city and we'll get this figured out. In the meantime, why don't you just meet with an oncologist at Dana-Farber just to be ready?" A meeting with an oncologist obviously fueled our anxiety, but the best information is key to any successful battle. It's probably just a precaution.

I vividly remember the first time I walked into Dana-Farber. Though not yet diagnosed with cancer, I recognized the gravity of the situation in which I found myself. Simply walking through the revolving doors of, arguably, the premier cancer institution of America, meant my life could be suddenly and dramatically changed. This consultation was not a second opinion on how best to cure a sagging chin line. This was serious – even at seventeen I felt the moment piling onto my shoulders.

The elevator doors closed behind us and we pressed the button for the pediatric unit. I had an urge to run screaming from the building with my arms waving wildly above my head. *"AAAAAAGH! I'm outta here!"* I didn't want to face someone in a white coat discussing survival rates for leukemia, lymphoma, myeloma, sarcoma or any other condition ending with a "ma". I just wanted to be sucking face with the hot senior cheerleader in my homeroom. The elevator slowed to a stop. Ding.

When the door opened we peered out apprehensively. I'd imagine my parents had no more desire to meet this cancer team than I did. We slowly stepped from the elevator and turned left. Walking down the corridor, I noticed a picture and plaque that are burned into my memory until this day. Every few weeks this image takes a running start from somewhere behind my brain stem and slams itself into the middle of my frontal lobe. A gentile twenty-something sits amiably for a portrait. His golden blonde hair frames a mostly unexceptional face. The two points that strike me are a pair of blue eyes brimming with intelligence and a smile that makes this boy look as if he's just gotten lucky.

Below the canvas is a plaque that describes the boy. He was a Harvard graduate who survived an initial bout of Lymphoma. After eight years in remission, his cancer returned. He didn't survive. His parents donated money – undoubtedly millions – to the Dana-Faber Cancer Institute pediatric unit. The portrait honors his memory and fight. To this day, his eyes, smile and story haunt me on a regular basis.

My mother pulled me past the plaque, thinking I was only stalling. We walked up to the receptionist, who greeted us with the usual pleasantries. After checking in, we sat in the waiting room. Two small, bald six-year-olds were playing the latest Nintendo video game on one of the televisions. I looked through children's magazines in quiet contempt and settled on a sports magazine likely present for impatient fathers.

After twenty minutes or so, the oncology nurse led us back to a clinical room. In reality, these rooms double for a second round waiting room. Just when you're about ready to get fed up waiting in the large comfortable waiting room of couches, TVs, and a plethora of magazines, a nurse calls your name. You're subsequently led into a smaller back room where, after a cursory temperature and blood-pressure check, you wait an eternity with one copy of Time magazine from four months prior.

Just before my father might have begun pacing the vinyl floor, the physician walked in. "Hello, My name is Dr. Shimbara," she announced. "And this is Dr. Sharp," she continued, pointing to the woman behind her.

Dr. Shimbara was a slightly built Asian woman in her early to mid-thirties, soft-spoken, but sure of herself. In contrast with some of the other physicians I'd met, her self-confidence didn't smack of ego or bravado. The other woman was older, white, and wore a pair of large-rimmed glasses that seemed to betray too many hours poring over medical texts. Dr. Shimbara went on to explain she would be our main point of contact, but Dr. Sharp would be a senior physician available to support and guide her.

The physicians quickly got down to business and began explaining how the cells of the Epstein Barre Virus (the cells that cause Mono) and Lymphoma appear amazingly similar under a microscope. The difficulty distinguishing between the cells was the cause of the long delay from the laboratories. Dr. Shimbara told us that the pathology slides had been sent to labs all over the city; Dana-Farber, Children's Hospital, Mass General Hospital, Brigham and Women's and Massachusetts Eye and Ear. The pathologists were having a difficult time deciding if what they were seeing were residual Epstein Barre cells from the prior infection or more ominous Lymphoma cells. No one wanted to make such a difficult call and be wrong so the slides traveled to many prestigious pathologists.

Dr. Shimbara explained that highly specific DNA tests were in process and we should know the outcome in another week or so. She also explained generally what might happen if the cells were cancerous and answered a few questions from my parents. I don't recall much of the meeting after the word "cancer." My trance was only broken when we rose to leave the hospital. We walked back out the revolving doors in silence and with more questions than we'd entered with.

During the ensuing weeks we lived in a constant fog of nervous anticipation. For my part, I was still fairly certain I didn't have cancer. I knew the results would pardon me and we could get back to life as normal. I still had face sucking to shoot for. As the weeks dragged into a month and beyond, I'd started to forget the news for which we were waiting. Then one day the phone rang.

It was a weekday at 5:30pm and the entire family was sitting down to dinner as we always do at that time of the evening. It was the beginning of winter and the frost was forming earlier each night, though we hadn't had our first snow yet. It was already dark outside and the steam from my mother's cooking had frozen upon the cold windowpanes and lent them an ethereal look. Moisture collected at the corners of windows and crept inward, slowly restricting vision to small circles.

We'd been discussing the day's events as usual.

"How was your day at work, dad?" I ventured.

"Ah, fine. Cold. How was school, did you two learn anything?"

"Nah, nuthin," I replied as though I was too cool for school.

I was already well into the start of senior year and had just been elected Social Chairperson of the class. The first order of business was to plan the senior prom. I also had a new girlfriend, Heather, and my dad was up to his usual jokes with that. Our dinner discussions were always spiced with just the right balance of humor, animosity, bickering and love. Dad was just starting to tease me about Heather when the telephone rang.

My mother got up to answer it because she sits the closest to the phone. As she answered it, she sat on the stool in front of the desk. Not breaking much of the conversation, we all looked at her out of curiosity regarding who had called. Who was it for? My hormones hoped it was a girl.

It was.

"Hello," my mother said politely.

"Oh, hi, Dr. Shimbara," she replies as she glances nervously at my father and me.

"Okay, well when did you find out?"

"Okay"

"Oh my God!"

As the conversation lengthened, my mother's cheeks grew mottled and blushed. Her voice grew nasally as her eyes welled with tears. I knew immediately something was wrong, and got a queasy feeling in the top of my stomach. It was sitting directly beneath my sternum and pressing inward.

The phone call was only lasted maybe five or six minutes at the most, but my life was irrevocably altered during that conversation. My mother continued to sniffle and release small sobs whilst Dr. Shimbara explained everything to her. Her fair skin reddened and betrayed her knowledge. As she hung up the phone her hands covered her moist cheeks.

The conversation at the table had stopped and we were wondering what Dr. Shimbara had told my mother. All the while we knew deep down what the news was. I felt the weight pushing on my chest. It was one of those things you already know the answer to, but ask with the hope that somehow, anyhow, your instincts have failed you this time. I thought maybe if I wished hard enough, my mother's response would be relatively benign compared to what I already knew she was going to say. Maybe I'm wrong. Maybe it's something else. Please dear God, let it be something else.

"What was that all about, mom?" I asked.

My mother walked over to my chair and knelt beside me.

"That was Dr. Shimbara from Dana-Farber", she said, as her eyes continued to well with tears. "She says they've finished the tests and have diagnosed you with Large-Celled Follicular Non-Hodgkin's Lymphoma. She wants to meet with us this week."

It is hard for me to describe in words how I felt at that moment. It felt so surreal. How clichéd, but truly, I felt strangely outside myself as though my mind was no longer part of my body. The body that had betrayed me.

I was absorbed in shock, I don't know how long I sat there until I spoke. I remember staring at my plate, my head slumped forward. Maybe, I thought, if I just concentrate on my food I wouldn't have to deal with it yet. We were eating mashed potatoes with applesauce spread over the top. The plates had little pink flowers around the rim. There was a small crack in one of the tiles that made up the tabletop. Mom always kept the kitchen magnificently clean, but she couldn't erase that small crack.

I wanted to stay in that trance to keep my mind from returning to reality and having to rationalize what was happening. I traced lined patterns into my potatoes and applesauce with my fork, across to the left, then back to the right, then up, down. I repeated the pattern over and over, wishing for some way to rewind time. Maybe I will wake up in a time before I had cancer. The Beatles song

"Yesterday" is sadly appropriate.

My mother leaned over and puts her arms around me. She was still sobbing. My father let out an inhumanly long sigh. It was a sigh you might release when you don't know what other sound to make and words do not seem appropriate in that moment. He reached over and put his large arm around me. My twelve-year-old sister just stared and cried. Dear God, what could she be thinking!
I was unable to cry. I was in too much shock. It just felt so damn unnatural. I was a teenager, invulnerable, invincible. This news went against everything I knew. Cancer could not happen to ME! I was seventeen and this kind of thing only happened to older people, not teenagers in the prime of life. I couldn't possibly have CANCER. I just had mono, how could that have anything to do with cancer? It was too much to comprehend all at once. I needed to stop thinking. I needed to get away!

After ten minutes of sitting in silence, I asked to be excused and walked down the hallway to my room. I had nothing more to say to my family and just needed to be alone for a while. It was nothing personal, but what do you say in such a situation? There is no real comfort to give when someone is confronted with such disturbing information. To say "I'm sorry" or "you'll be okay" is felt trite. I needed to hurt on my own for a while. I was mad.

I was confused. I felt as if I had been cast away to a remote island where no one could comfort me.

I sat on my bed bewildered by what I had just been told. I tried to absorb it for a while; eventually it sank in. I did what most seventeen-year-old boys might do. I picked up the phone and called, Heather. I began to explain to her what was going on. And that was when the tears finally came. I began to sob, as did she. I realized this was the beginning of a long and tiring journey. I could feel the devastation welling up in the spot in my chest, the pain growing. Inside me grew a cesspool of anger, bewilderment, uncertainty, and fear. The feelings slowly rose to the surface, like a toilet refills itself, the emotions swirling in and around each other.

For her part, Heather told me everything was going to be alright and promised she would stick by me and help me through. I respected her decision immensely, but wasn't sure I wanted her to have to deal with it as well. I wasn't sure how I was going to manage this horrific adventure so I wasn't sure it was fair to drag Heather along with me. We were both only in high school and neither of us had developed the mental and emotional fortitude to deal with anything of this magnitude. I told her right then and there that if she wanted out I would understand – and I meant it. She said she wasn't going anywhere. And she didn't.

Over the course of the next two weeks, my father took several days off work and we drove the hour back and forth to Boston to talk with Dr. Shimbara. We talked with her about what the next steps would be, about a prognosis, and what I could expect. She told us I had Large-celled Follicular Non-Hodgkin's Lymphoma and that she'd presented my situation to the team of doctors at Dana-Farber who were overlooking my case. Yet, this team of world expert did not know what to do. This was the first time they had encountered this type of Lymphoma in someone so young.

"It's a forty year old's disease," Dr. Shimbara told us, "not a seventeen year old's." Actually, it's the same form of Lymphoma that Massachusetts Senator Paul Tsongas succumbed to. There was no precedent for an effective chemotherapy regimen in someone my age.

They aren't sure what to do yet? This is one of the leading cancer research institutions in the entire world and they do not know what to do. What the HELL do you mean they aren't sure what to do yet!?

Lymphoma is a general term for a group of cancers that originate in the lymphatic system. The system is made up of thin tubes that branch into the body's tissues. Their primary purpose is to manage fluids within the body, filter bacteria and house white blood cells. Located along this network are small bean-shaped organs called lymph nodes. Clusters of these lymph nodes are found in the underarm, groin, neck, and abdomen, the places your doctor palpates to see if you're sick or not. Other parts of the lymphatic system include the spleen, thymus, tonsils, and bone marrow. Lymphoma results when a lymphocyte, a type of white blood cell that travels in this lymphatic network, undergoes a change and begins to multiply uncontrollably. At its core, this is essentially what cancer is – a set of cells that have mutated and can't shut down one of their systems or stop multiplying. The malignant cells eventually crowd out healthy cells and create tumors that enlarge the lymph nodes and other sites in the body. The most common warning sign of non-Hodgkin's lymphoma is a painless swelling of a lymph node or nodes. My swollen tonsils may have been the first presentation of a tumor, in which case we were lucky to catch it so early. Wait, lucky to catch a tumor? Yeah, what an auspicious stroke of luck.

To lend some perspective on the extent of these diseases, the American Cancer Society reports that, in 2016, 14.5 million people were living with a history of cancer in the United States. 1.7 million people were expected to be diagnosed and 595,690 are expected to die in the same year. That's 1,632 people each day. This disease is amazingly pervasive. In the US, men have about a one in two lifetime risk of developing cancer, and for women the risk is one in three. Cancer is the second leading cause of death in the United States after heart disease.

The fantastic news is that the 5-year relative survival rate for all cancers diagnosed 2005-2011 was 69%. This is up significantly from 49% during 1975-1977. This improvement is due to both advances in treatment but also increases in screening and earlier diagnosis

While cancer affects many Americans, my case was extremely rare. Non-Hodgkin's lymphoma is the sixth most common, yet second fastest growing, cancer in the United States today. About 81,080 Americans will be diagnosed with lymphoma in 2016. The incidence of non-Hodgkin's lymphoma rose by 80 percent from 1973 to 1997 - an annual percentage increase of nearly three percent. Approximately 300,000 people in the US are living with non-Hodgkin's lymphoma; about 1 in 100. Fortunately, survival for all invasive childhood cancers combined has improved markedly over the past 30 years due to new and improved treatments. The 5-year relative survival rate increased from 58% in the mid-1970s to 70% in 2016.

The US also has around 1700 children under the age of twenty diagnosed with lymphoma each year. 750 to 800 cases are non-Hodgkin's lymphoma. My case of Non-Hodgkin's Large-Celled Follicular Lymphoma was the first and only case the world had known in an adolescent at the time. I was special indeed.

Like mine, most cases of lymphoma are idiopathic. The word idiopathic means, "arising spontaneously or from an obscure or unknown cause".

You mean to tell me you don't know how I got cancer? You don't know why my body is killing me? The cause is "idiopathic"? What does that mean?

It is a word used to cover innumerable medical problems. It's quite a convenient word – created by a profession swathed in science. Medicine is a field grounded in biology, pharmacology, and most importantly, terminology.

Fancy Latin names describe diseases that lead to disability and death. Yet for all the science, the cause for far too many diseases is "idiopathic" – unknown. "Mr. Roderick, I'm afraid we do not understand why you have cancer or where it came from. But we think that chemotherapy might cure it."

All of these mysterious origins wouldn't be so hard to swallow if the collective ego of the healthcare system was able to simply admit a lack of knowledge.

In previous generations, it might have been beneficial to keep patients in the dark. Their physician struggled with uncertainty in the comfort of his own office and eventually came to a conclusion of the diagnosis and an appropriate treatment. The patient trusted this learned doctor and followed orders religiously. With fewer effective medicinal or surgical treatments available, it was unnecessary to provide patients with alternatives. However, in our Internet age, with proliferating sources of information, the healthcare field has been unable to hide their shortcomings. I'm generalizing of course, but too often patients aren't provided with all the options they might wish for. Shorter and shorter appointments prevent physicians from engaging in the kinds of discussions about medical treatments that both patients and physicians might like to hold to make the most appropriate decisions. Instead, our doctors are forced to make paternalistic decisions on our behalf, often with very little input from us.

Let me be fair. Physicians spend a significant part of their adult lives learning about medicine to help people live a longer and healthier life. Fortunately for us, they are trained to assess a patient's symptoms, identify the most likely problem, and prescribe a solution. Their vast knowledge helps countless people survive countless diseases every day. However, swamped with HMO paperwork and bills to pay, no doctor can remain abreast of every advancement in his or her field. There will always be a gap between what is currently known in the healthcare universe and what one particular physician will have learned.

As patients continue to arrive at their doctor's appointments with reams of internet printouts, physicians may be forced to admit the extent of their knowledge. Clearly an internet search can turn up plenty of misinformation and patients may be unable to discern fact from fiction. However, more resources are devoted to clear and truthful health information each year. "Doctor's orders" may someday be replaced by "Doctor's options". They are after all, only human. Human is not such a bad thing for a physician to be.

In his book, One Hundred Days, Dr. David Biro writes, "My situation, in fact, is by no means unique in the annals of medicine. Physicians are faced with irresolvable problems all the time.

Medicine, even in the age of molecular biology and the Human Genome Project, no matter how much the lay public would like to believe otherwise, is still more art than science." This is why we call it the medical "practice."

So, the practicing oncologists told me that I was a "special" patient, but I didn't feel very special. I didn't look forward to being experimented on. I wanted a quick and decisive solution to the cancerous cells attacking my body. I was no longer waging war against a virus, this was my own body, but I demanded the same outcome. I wanted the rogue cells destroyed. I didn't expect to hear, "we're not sure what to do yet." I had not planned for that scenario.

However, planned or not, we still faced a dilemma. There were no known cases of this cancer in a person my age. Surely my case was special, but it was not easy. As scientific as we imagine it all to be, there will always be new cases that have not been treated before. The oncologists viewed this case in an academic and intellectual sense. In some small way, my screwed up immune system was expanding the knowledge base of medicine. The team at Dana-Farber would design a protocol that they hoped would work, and then simply try it out. My lymphoma would either respond to the chemotherapy regimen they designed or it wouldn't. Either way, the scientific community would have another data point to inform future decisions. This is the basis for medicine. All science, including medicine, is based on "trial and error". I just hoped I'd wind up with less of the "error" part.

Chapter 6

I now shouldered the burden of explaining to my friends that I had cancer. I remember the overwhelming feelings of fear and apprehension that foreshadowed many of their reactions. My seventeen-year-old imagination invented horrible visions of the faces people would make, the words they would whisper behind my back, the way they would step out of my way in the high school hallways. In my mind, a leper would have received a warmer welcome in my high school.

Crap, how am I going to tell them what is going on? I have cancer and I'm sure none of them want to deal with that. They'll probably just pretend I'm invisible so that they don't have to acknowledge this horrible disease. What will the GIRLS think?! This is going to be awful.

Much to my surprise, the reactions from my friends were mostly positive. The few people I told were immensely supportive. Some reacted awkwardly at first, but were universally willing to help in any way possible. Teacher and school administrators at the high school in Wareham, Massachusetts went out of their way to assure my parents I would be taken care of in school. They promised to allow me to miss days when needed and to create homework that would allow me to keep up with my peers. Their response gave me a great foundation from which I could begin to figure out how to fight the cancer. With so many people in my corner, I had no choice but to buckle down and work through the issues at hand. I had cancer and needed to decide how I was going to deal with it.

We began meeting regularly with Dr. Shimbara in her Boston office. She first attempted to figure out how the cancer started. Idiopathic origin aside, Dr. Shimbara and her team surmised that perhaps the massive Epstein-Barre infection caused a malignancy in one of my lymphocytes. The cell was damaged and couldn't stop reproducing itself. Fatefully, it grew within my neck. One cell created two. Two cells created an army. Before I knew it, we received that phone call. "Mrs. Roderick, it appears that Kyle has something wrong. We believe it's large-celled follicular lymphoma."

Dr. Shimbara did extensive research and eventually the team of doctors designed a protocol for my treatment. It would require five months of high dose chemotherapy. Now, chemotherapy is some nasty stuff. Basically, the chemicals are designed to target and kill all of the fast-growing cells in a person's body, such as cancer cells. The drugs kill or damage cancer cells so that they cannot reproduce. Because chemotherapy affects all systems in the body, it is called "systemic" therapy. Patients receive treatment at regular intervals, as inpatients or outpatients, usually over several months. The chemotherapy continues to work for days or weeks after the drugs are taken.

Unfortunately, while chemotherapy does such a great job at stopping the reproduction of growing cells, they aren't the only fast growing cells in our bodies. These toxic chemicals affect hair cells, white and red blood cells, platelets, and reproductive organs. Dr. Shimbara explained to me that I would get six doses of CHOP chemotherapy, one dose every three weeks. The name comes from the four drugs that are used in the CHOP regimen; cyclophosphamide, Adriamycin, oncovin, and prednisone. I'm not sure where the "H" went.

    Several tests were taken prior to me starting chemo so they could get a baseline of my body functions before they started pumping poisons into my body. I had hearing tests, vision tests, EKGs for my heart, CT scans to search for other tumors, and many others. All of these were relatively benign. A pressure cuff here, a beep there, an electrode on that arm, a needle prick in the other. Of course, you wouldn't expect it to be that easy right. Of course not.

    There was the small task of testing my bone marrow. They wanted to rule out the possibility of malignancy in the marrow. I went to Dana-Farber to have the procedure done. A male physician in his early forties led me into the surgical room. He dimmed the lights to keep me calm and my mother sat down on a stainless steel stool. He instructed me to lay face down on the flat vinyl table. I did as he asked and rested my chin on interwoven fingers. In front of me was a counter with a sink, and cabinets full of syringes, needles and other instruments of torture. The doctor asked me to pull my athletic pants halfway down my buttocks. The ignoble procedure was fairly routine at the clinic and there was no air of importance on his part – all part of a day's work. I on the other hand was scared to death. I'm sure he was perfectly nice, but the procedure was feeling a bit "horror movie torture scene" at this point.

The doctor called in a nurse to assist him and prepared for the biopsy. He made some small talk, of which I have no recollection. Thankfully, she seemed a bit more empathetic. She knew what was about to happen. After preparing his tray of metal instruments, he was ready to begin. The nurse wiped my exposed rear hip, above my right butt cheeks, with an iodine-soaked gauze pad to sterilize the area. She then wiped it clean with an alcohol pad. "Hey, look, instant tan!" I thought.

As the nurse prepared the area, my mother rounded the table and stood in front of me. She offered to hold my hand, which I did more for her comfort than mine. This won't be that bad. I've dealt with pain before. Then, the evil "Dr. Feelbad" then raised a small needle and tested the syringe. A small amount of lidocaine jumped from the end of his needle in a large arch. The stream reminded me of Mannekin Pis, the Belgian sculpture of a boy nonchalantly peeing into a fountain.

The doctor mindlessly began his routine with little hesitation. The cool of the evaporating alcohol was replaced by a warmer sensation where the needle entered. There seemed to be only the slightest prick as the lidocaine needle pierced my skin. Soon, the skin above my hip was nonexistent. This won't be so bad; I can't even feel the skin. Yet, I cringed as I watched him pick up the next instrument. Shiny stainless steel, ten inches long. It was not thin, it was not small – it was nothing short of massive!

With no fanfare, the doctor quickly jabbed it into my flesh, which was fortunately anesthetized. As it struck home, he grunted as he pushed it into my bone. Technically, he was aiming to push through the rear hipbone, or iliac crest, where a large quantity of bone marrow is located. As he forced the steel through my bone, he employed a twisting motion to help him dig deeper. I won't over exaggerate, at this point, the pain is not excruciating. It hurts, but the actual bone has no nerve endings – only the tissues surrounding the bone.

Still, the sound of the twisting needle grinding on my bones made me sick to my stomach. I heard my mother sniffle and an "Oh God" escaped her lips. I did not dare to look, but knew her face was turning red. I heard her crying. Metal scraped on bone. The pain caused my grip to tighten around mom's hand but I resisted squeezing harder, fearing I'd hurt her.

As the needle finally popped through the outer bone and into the marrow, Dr. Feelbad pulled back on the syringe. Now the grinding was really bad, and as he extracted small amounts of the marrow, waves of pain coursed through my body. That did hurt - to my core! My entire body jerked with each pull of the syringe and I squeezed my mother's hand until it was bloodless.

"Almost done," Feelbad grunted.

A few more pulls, a few more jumps and it was over. My brow was damp with sweat and my mother's cheeks were wet with tears; but it was over. There were no surgical incisions or stitches involved - only skin punctures where the needle had been inserted. One small hole cannot symbolize the pain I went through that afternoon.

Not long afterwards, Dr. Shimbara handed me a large booklet of possible side effects and explained, "Nobody gets all of the side effects, but everybody gets some of them." She was preparing me for the ordeal of chemotherapy. After reading this great big book of possible side effects, I was one scared seventeen-year-old. I read about all the consequences of chemotherapy. Side effects included, but was not limited to; loss of hair, fatigue, irritability, loss of concentration, nausea, vomiting, loss of appetite, loss of weight. Even death got a mention.

Wait, they "include but are not limited to death?" What the hell ARE they limited to?

I was completely unprepared to contemplate the possibility of heart disease, irreversible liver damage, fatal allergies, severe hearing loss, brain damage and most devastating to me: infertility. Infertility? Are you kidding me?! I had never doubted the fact that I wanted children in my life and now that option, that most amazing of human experiences, was being denied to me. I could wind up a vegetable, contentedly dribbling pureed peas down my chin, or live twenty more years but without the ability to have children. And this is supposed to save my life?

It seemed I had no choice. I was angry and devastatingly powerless. I couldn't forego treatment just because of the possibility of side effects. However, the thought of growing up brain damaged, deaf and without children didn't thrill me either. I had no control over my body, no control of my future. But as they say, the show must go on. Feelings are not included in the protocol.

The chemotherapy started a few weeks later at Dana-Faber Cancer Institute. I was scared. Even after reading all the books and warnings, I walked into that clinic unclear about what to expect. The pamphlets listed side effect charts, but no words can capture the full experience of going through chemotherapy. Realize that whenever a person talks about the experience, they refer to it as "going through" chemotherapy. When you take antibiotics, get x-rayed, have surgery, you go through chemotherapy.

My mother and Aunt Claire accompanied me to the hospital for that first infusion. A nurse led us down the hallway and into a large room in the back of the pediatric clinic. We were given our own little corner. Various compartments were separated by the standard off-white sheets suspended from the ceiling. They gave a superficial feeling of privacy. There were individual televisions for each patient's chair, and one large television with a VCR on the far side of the room, bolted to the wall. Walking into that room for the first time was disturbing. It was unsettling to see pale, weak, underweight, bald children hooked up to these bags of synthetic chemicals. I walked into that room as a relatively healthy teenager and these children vividly predicted my future. The sterile white walls and bright fluorescent lights gave an unfamiliar glow that overwhelmed me. They lit up my own personal hell and sectioned it off with sheets hung from the ceiling.

As we began, the nurses had trouble getting the IV started properly. After a few unsuccessful attempts, they eventually found a good vein. Finally, the chemo bags were hung, and I watched the first poisonous drops travel through the plastic tubing, through the needle and into my arm. I didn't feel any different. I'm not sure what I expected, but I didn't feel much at all initially. I could hear the humming of the mechanical pump as it infused these chemicals into my bloodstream. Click, whooooosh. Click, whoooooosh. Click, whoooooosh. The plastic tubing danced rhythmically as it shook each time the machine forced the fluids through the hoses and into my veins.

At first, there were a flurry of doctors and nurses there to make sure I wasn't having any allergic reactions, and my vital signs were monitored very closely. However, the bulk of the day turned out to be ironically uneventful. The first sign I noticed was when I went into the bathroom for the first time at the end of the afternoon. As I peed into the toilet, I was shocked to watch the bowl turn red! I'm peeing cherry Kool-Aid! I can't believe my urine is actually this red! One of the drugs they had given me was bright red in the bag, and here I was pissing it out. We're talking candy apple, Crayola® red here. This experience, while odd, was my first realization that these chemicals were truly coursing through my body.

It wasn't until the third day that I truly noticed the effects of the drugs. By that time, the chemo had hopefully killed all the cancerous cells roaming free in my lymphatic system. The toxins also began to attack my healthy blood cells as well. I grew weaker, my body was more susceptible to infection and a low platelet count could lead to internal bleeding.

These chemicals were destroying everything that reproduced rapidly, friend or foe. This included all my blood cells. The body constantly produces new blood cells. In healthy adults, an estimated 100 billion red cells and 400 million white cells are produced each hour. The life span of mature blood cells is short - only a few days or months. To the chemotherapeutic agents, they behaved much like cancer cells.

Red blood cells (erythrocytes) make up forty five percent of blood volume. Their primary function is to pick up oxygen in the lungs and transport it to tissues and other organs throughout the body. At the tissue level, red blood cells exchange oxygen for carbon dioxide and carry it back to the lungs to be exhaled. Damage to these cells caused me to feel tired and lightheaded. My body was heavy and I had trouble concentrating.

White blood cells (leukocytes) are outnumbered by red blood cells by a margin of one for every 1,000. There are five main types of white cells: neutrophils (also called granulocytes), eosinophils, basophils, monocytes, and lymphocytes. Each plays a distinct and important role in helping the immune system fight infection. My doctors believed that during the horrible fight with mono, a damaged lymphocyte multiplied and became the lymphoma we were now fighting. Lymphocytes are the smallest white blood cells and are the backbone of the immune system. They fight viral infections and assist in the destruction of other parasites, bacteria and fungi. One group of lymphocytes called *T-cells* regulates the immune system's response to invading organisms and is the body's main defense against viruses and protozoa. A second group called *B-cells* manufactures a kind of protein called an antibody or immunoglobulin. Antibodies attach to the surface of foreign organisms or the cells they have invaded and summon a group of proteins in the bloodstream called The Complement System to surround the infected organism or cell and dissolve a hole in it in order to kill it. As the chemotherapy damaged these cells, it caused my immune system to weaken. Dr. Shimbara explained that I must be hyper-vigilant to remain healthy. I had to get enough rest, eat well and remain obsessively hygienic to stave off any possibility of infection.

Thrombocytes (platelets) are the smallest cell elements in the bloodstream. Platelets primarily control bleeding. Without platelets, my body would lack the ability to clot blood if a vessel was damaged. A fall off a bicycle could cause massive internal bleeding that my body would be unprepared to stop. Luckily, I was too tired to ride.

I began to feel weaker with each passing day and I knew that my immune system was now fully compromised. As each day progressed the fatigue grew and I often felt faint. My arms and legs grew heavier and my mind was cloudy. Something was happening inside my body and it didn't feel like a "cure" at all. About two weeks after the first infusion, just as I began to wonder if the lethargy would ever pass, my stamina began to improve. I slowly began to notice an improvement in my energy, concentration and mood. At the three-week mark, I felt just about back to normal - just in time for the next round of chemotherapy.

To say it was not a pleasant experience is an understatement. Something was terribly wrong deep within my body. I had never felt anything like this before and I was intensely scared. As a teenager, I was becoming aware of how to deal with the changes in my body. But there was something too abstract, too intangible about the effects chemotherapy had on my body. I was unable to fight the venom that made me feel so terrible. All I could do was acquiesce. I felt like I had no control over my body, no control over the place where my thoughts and feelings resided. Many adolescents hate their bodies. Angry or confused over changes that take place, we stare endlessly into mirrors hoping to figure it all out. My thoughts were different. I hated my body for betraying me. I hated it for making me feel so weak. I hated it for forcing me to think about mortality. I wished I could be a normal teen boy again because I could totally deal with ill-timed erections. That'd be a cake walk compared to the horror I was experiencing.

In an act of defiance and self-control, and a touch of denial, I chose to stay in school even on days when I should have stayed in bed. I showed up to advanced placement and honors classes as well as after school activities. I did my homework. I had already informed most of my teachers and some of my closest friends soon after I was diagnosed, but had decided not to make my condition common knowledge. I was fearful that many of my friends and peers wouldn't know how to approach me. Perhaps they'd respond with compassion and empathy, but perhaps it would be with anxiety and apprehension. I was sure that I could survive without much help and I could avoid pity or trepidation.

Time has afforded me the perspective to understand that these thoughts were foolish. In an attempt to prove my valor, I forced myself to endure days in a socially complex high school environment when I needed to let my body rest. Some days the bell sounded the end of class and I had no recollection of the lesson. One day, as I was walking up the stairs, I fainted. I fell backwards. Fortunately a fellow student caught me and pushed me back up.

"You alright, man?" he said with concern.

"Yeah, yeah, I'm fine, I'm fine . . . Thanks."

"You almost fell down the stairs, man! You don't seem alright."

"I know, I know . . . thanks a lot for catching me. Thanks." I caught my breath and slinked away.

    I continued to attend school as often as possible to prove to myself it wasn't such a big deal, and I wasn't really facing a life-threatening experience. I tried hard to avoid using the word "cancer" when describing my ordeal. Invariably the cancer was called "my illness," or "I'm sick" but the word "cancer" hardly ever came out of my mouth. After the "Why me?" stage, it was a rapid transition into denial. I pretended I wasn't really dealing with cancer. At some points it was a healthy dose of denial. Refusing to acknowledge the seriousness of my diagnosis allowed me to focus on maintaining a positive outlook. My mother admonished me constantly for not incorporating the cancer into every detail of my life. Surely there were times when I should have respected more reasonable limitations based on my body's weakened immune system. But denial was an important weapon against my disease. At times, it helped keep me sane.

    Like many cancer patients, I viewed my predicament as a battle to be fought and won. But I felt it was a battle to fight on my own. What I didn't recognize at the time was the many soldiers on the flank willing to help me fight. What I realize now, is that in the effort to spare my friends their offer of support, I robbed them of the chance to help someone they cared about. It was not an obligation for them, but a show of love and respect. I wish I'd had the maturity and foresight to accept their help. It is amazing how supportive people can be if you give them the chance. Yet, in my quiet stoicism I remained as nervous as everyone else and I simply wouldn't acknowledge it.

It was my behavior at home with my family that I regret most. Because I didn't allow anyone to talk openly about my health, we lived in a household lined with eggshells and landmines. No one was free to discuss how they felt or express their frustrations and fears. Yet they all had their own stresses outside my illness. Such is life. As I remained silent about my feelings, my family and friends felt unable to complain about anything else that might seem trivial in comparison. It didn't ease their burden to see me struggle stoically. Instead, it pained them more. In particular, I think about Dana.

My sister was strangely quiet about her feelings towards my illness and it worried us tremendously. She was ten when I was diagnosed with lymphoma, and being such an intelligent child, I have no doubt she recognized immediately the seriousness of the situation. I'm sure she was scared that she might lose her big brother. I rarely had the chance to speak with her about it and she said very little. She didn't ask questions. Perhaps my unwillingness to express negative emotions set precedence for her. However, the situation clearly affected her deeply.

One evening, while passing past her bedroom, I heard a sniffle. I took a few quiet steps back and peered through the crack in the door and saw my sister sitting under the purple satin canopy of her bed. She was crying. She was sitting upright grasping her legs, her face buried into her knees. What is she crying for? Nothing had happened, nothing had changed. I assumed she was crying simply because she was afraid. She didn't want me to die. What must have been going through her head as I was at the hospital all the time? Did she imagine a world without me in it? I slowly opened her bedroom door and poked my head in with a smile.

"Can I come in?" I asked softly.

"Mmm hmm," she replied.

"Why are you crying?"

She shrugged her shoulders, but didn't look up.

"Is everything okay," I asked, trying to get her to open up.

I couldn't tell if she just shrugged again or shook her head to indicate yes or no.

"Dana, you know I'm going to be all right, right?" I managed to say, trying hard to sound sure of myself. "I promise, I'm going to be alright. I love you."
She lifted her arms to hug me and held on for a long time. She said nothing.

Now, while most of our exchanges were subtle and loving, I must admit that sibling rivalry also played a factor in the equation. In the war for attention, my cancer dropped the atomic bomb on Dana's efforts. Everyone was so intently focused on supporting a quiet and angry Kyle, that Dana was pushed to the margins on many days. While I received dozens of get-well cards, presents and phone calls every day, Dana felt neglected. Clearly, no one meant to ignore her. In fact, I don't think that's what truly happened, but while I received lots of special attention she didn't. My silence only fueled my family's efforts to support me. As a typical ten year old, this must have secretly burned a hole in Dana's self-perception.

    As the school year progressed, so too did my rounds of chemotherapy. Every three weeks I traveled back to Dana-Farber for additionally chemotherapy treatments. After the second and third doses, my hair began to fall out and it started to become noticeable. Each shower washed more hair down the bathtub drain. Each morning the sun rose to illuminate fine hairs on my pillow and in my bed. The effects of the chemotherapy were becoming painfully, outwardly, obvious. The loss of hair can be difficult for any cancer patient. On one hand, there are issues surrounding the social acceptance of baldness and feelings of self-consciousness in public. Surely, there is an issue of vanity, even in an atmosphere of survival. Remember that I was a teenage American boy beginning to ogle at the Victoria's Secret catalogue. Survival wasn't my only concern.

    However, baldness is much more difficult to cancer patients because it is the foremost outward sign that there is something seriously wrong with you. It serves as an unwanted proclamation of a very private and troubling issue to anyone who can see your head. There is no other disease whose cure will make your hair fall out, so even perfect strangers become aware of an extremely personal issue. That's why so many cancer patients invest money in wigs, hats, and scarves for their heads. It's not simply about looking better; it's about looking normal so that everyone around you doesn't have a window into your private problems. I didn't want pity. I didn't want to be on show.

In one respect, I was lucky. In our society, it is much easier to become a bald man than a bald woman. I decided to use this to my advantage and employed a sort of Jujitsu. I shaved my head before most of my hair fell out. I'd finally found something I'd been searching for, a way of fighting back. I would not allow my bald head to pronounce "cancer patient" to the world. John Q. Public would not know of my war yet. So one night, Heather and I lathered up my head with shaving cream and shaved every bit of hair with a disposable blue Bic razor. The shaving cream dripped down the sides of my face and the blade dug into my skin, but I was fighting back. My cancerous anonymity may not last forever, but perhaps this would stall the pity party. As Heather scratched the razor over my scalp, I watched.

What the hell am I doing? Why am I shaving my head? I still couldn't believe I had cancer despite how it had changed so many things about my life. I didn't want to be pitied, but I WAS scared.

My plan was not infallible. Everyone in school saw that one day I had hair, and the next day I didn't, so of course it was talked about. Even with email, word travels faster in the hallways of a high school than an electronic network. So I picked a story and stuck by it.

"Why did you shave your head?" they might ask.

"Ah, I just wanted a new look," I practiced with an Oscar-winning smile.

And it worked! Hardly anyone in the school, save the teachers and my close friends, knew what I was going through. They saw me in school almost every day and just figured I shaved my head to stand out. Luckily, my eyebrows and eyelashes remained intact. Everything else, everything, was gone. The shower collected hair after hair, but fate allowed me to keep my eyebrows and continue my bald imitation for the duration of the experience.

However, having a bald head wasn't completely painless. I remember one specific incident in the high school cafeteria, when I'd gotten into line for lunch. The lunch ladies always loved me because they thought I was just the most polite young man. I asked them about their families and how their day was going, and so we talked every day. A few days after I had shaved my head, one of the women looked at me oddly from beneath her hair net, "Oh my! Now, why did you shave your head?" She asked with contempt.

"You're such a nice boy, you shouldn't have shaved your head. You looked so nice with hair . . ."

It was a vivid reminder that I could fool the high school, but not escape my reality. The reality was that if chemotherapy was destroying my hair follicles, it surely was tearing my insides to pieces. The reality was that if the chemotherapy didn't work, I was going to die. I was trying to escape this prison of truth and didn't want anyone to question me or talk about it. Shaved head or not, I still had cancer.

There were many times when I was out with my family, or Heather, or friends and got strange looks from people. I was convinced they were trying to figure out if I had shaved my head to look like Michael Jordan, or if I was undergoing chemotherapy. Surely they saw past my charade. It seemed they would look at me puzzled, trying to guess. I was self-conscious about it, I mean, who really wants to be bald unless they shave their head on purpose? I just tried to always act like I did it to look different, but the truth was, I didn't want to look different.

Tears replaced the hairs on my pillow. My hair couldn't fall out anymore, but I felt like I was falling apart.

The rest of my senior year went by as smoothly as possible, I suppose. The chemo treatments continued every month as planned but I refused to lose hope. As part of my denial, I refused to believe that I would not be able to go to college. I began the process of filling out applications and visiting colleges. Both anxiety and excitement grew as I read through brochure after brochure. My parents and I went on college visiting tours and researched extensively. Finally, after all the looking, I found the perfect place. I was invited to spend four days at a college in the woods to explore what they had to offer. The lush green grass and historic brick buildings conjured images of an amazing college experience. I looked at a number of schools, but after the four days I spent visiting Dartmouth College in beautiful rural Hanover, New Hampshire, I knew it was the perfect place for me. I sent my application away and hoped their admissions board would choose me as a student.

Time passed and I continued to go to school every single day and made trips to Boston every other week for checkups or for chemotherapy treatments. The hospital appointments sailed along without any abnormal complications for a few months. Overall, things weren't terribly bad. Months two, three and four came and went and other than sleepless nights and a serious lack of energy, I didn't feel too badly.

However, toward the end of the five-month regimen, the nurses and doctors began to worry about the condition of my veins. Before I started chemotherapy, the oncologist asked me if I would allow her to put a porta-catheter in my chest. A porta catheter (more commonly called a port) is a device implanted in the chest that gives the physicians easier access to a patient's bloodstream. With a port, the nurses wouldn't need to start the IV in my arm each time. When Dr. Shimbara brought up this idea, she told me the main reasons were to avoid the discomfort of having a needle constantly stuck in my arm, but also because one of the drugs they were administering would cause irreparable harm if it leaked into my muscle tissue. If the IV wasn't inserted directly into the vein, or if it shifted during an infusion, this particular chemical would cause severe third degree chemical burns beneath my skin.

I objected to the port. I felt that having a permanent reminder of my illness would only make things more difficult. My mother argued with me. Dr. Shimbara argued with me. They wanted me to be as safe as possible. But neither of them could understand what was going on in my head. I didn't want to be in the shower or getting dressed and see or feel a foreign object in my chest. I felt like that damn piece of plastic would just be mocking me. I pictured it staring back from the mirror with delight. I had spent a tremendous amount of time constructing my fortress and thinking about the cancer as little as possible. I wouldn't allow them to brand me with a reminder of my condition. Hell, I was already bald wasn't I?

So the doctors and nurses were just cautious with the IVs and eventually I reached round six. Ding! Ding! Ding! The bell rang to sound the end of the fight – and I was still standing. It was time to go to the judges' scorecards. More waiting and hoping were in order, but at least I'd made it this far. After the denial phase, cancer was finally incorporated into my developing self-image. I was a fighter. I was a guy who had fought cancer and was still alive. Only time could reveal the real victor.

Chapter 7

"Everyone's future is, in reality, an urn full of unknown treasures from which all may draw unguessed prizes."

- Lord Dunsany

After the chemotherapy, the rest of my senior year was passing quite easily. My energy was slowly returning and my hair even began to grow back. I took on more responsibilities and gradually my mother stopped hovering over me like an injured animal. I began performing usual activities, I planned the senior prom and bugged my little sister. Day by day, I was becoming normal again. I even started hearing from universities. I began receiving acceptance letters shortly after finishing the last rounds of chemotherapy. Hearing from almost every other school, I anxiously awaited word from Dartmouth, my first choice. Letters had come from many other schools I had applied to – except the one I truly *wanted*.

One spring day, as I arrived home from school, I walked through the back door of our home and into the kitchen. My mother was standing in the middle of the room, to the left of the kitchen table, her face flushed and sniffling. I recognized immediately that she'd been crying. My sister was crouched behind our blue velvet couch - a feeble attempt to hide. The scenario seemed quite odd to me, almost comical, and I wondered what in the world was going on. Obviously, I asked what was wrong, but my mother only told me that the mail had come. She then handed me a small envelope from Harvard University.

Every high school senior knows that the size of the envelope is an easy indicator as to whether you'd been accepted to a school or not. Clearly, I had not been accepted to Harvard, but as I opened it, I told my mother it was okay. I hadn't actually loved my tour at Harvard anyway. Then she started sniffling and handed me a big white envelope from Dartmouth College. I knew right away it was an acceptance letter, and my sister jumped up from the couch and took a photograph as my mother threw her arms around my neck.

"I'm so happy for you, Kyle! I'm so (sniff) happy for you!"

In the photograph Dana snapped, I have the biggest, most satisfied smile on my face as I read the letter of acceptance. I already knew my decision. I was heading to Hanover.

To conclude the rollercoaster ride of my senior year, fate threw one last curveball my way. A special invitation arrived in my mailbox informing my family that I was getting an award at the Seniors Award Ceremony. I assumed I'd won some dork award or something. The ceremony seemed to drag on with awards for perfect attendance. In the middle of the event, I was called for maintaining the highest average in one of my classes. Won't this thing ever end, I thought. The night seemed to drag on forever, and as a teenager anxiously approaching my final summer, I had places to go, people to see. I was a mover and shaker and felt the world might just stop spinning if I didn't get out of that auditorium in time.

The last award of the evening was the Principal's Award. Principal Dan Burke walked up on stage and slowly approached the podium. Over the course of the year, Mr. Burke and I had grown to be pretty friendly. Principal Burke is a rotund, jovial man who speaks and walks very slowly, but with meaning. He is the kind of man who chooses his words carefully and means each one he says. He also cared about his students very much. I'll never forget the time he came all the way to Children's Hospital to visit me during my battle with mono to deliver a roast beef sub. "Kyle, I hear the food in these places is terrible. I thought you might like this sandwich from my favorite sub shop," he'd said. Unfortunately, my throat was still too sore to eat it, but man did it smelled delicious!

After he'd adjusted the microphone on stage, Mr. Burke began to speak.

"Ladies and gentlemen, I'd like to tell you a little about the recipient this year's Principal's Award. This student has been an inspiration to us this year. His courage and perseverance has been a lesson to us all."

As Mr. Burke continued to describe the recipient, my family and classmates all recognized he was talking about me. He described someone with toughness and determination. He explained what an inspiration it was to have a student in the school who faced such terrible odds with bravery and stoicism. He explained how worried he'd been for my health, yet how I always smiled when he saw me.

I couldn't believe he was talking about me. I'd never thought of myself as brave before. Stoic, sure. I knew I'd been pig-headed about that, but "brave"? It lent a new vision of myself to hear him speak such kind words in front of all those people. When he was done, he called me up on stage to accept the "Principal's Award for Courage." The whole auditorium rose to their feet and gave me an ovation I will never forget. There was hardly a dry eye in the joint as I made my way up the stairs toward the podium. Teachers, family members, classmates and friends cheered me on and kept clapping as I approached Principal Burke.

As I took each step closer to the stage, an evolution took place. This was the first time I began to realize what I had truly done - and I was proud! I had survived a tremendous challenge. I finally realized how many obstacles I had overcome. Not only had I proven the oncologists wrong and graduated on time, but I had good grades and had been accepted to an Ivy-League college.

I reached the stage and desperately tried to stave off tears as I walked toward Principal Burke. When I got to the podium, he wrapped my hand in his and smiled as he announced the deepest-felt "congratulations" I'd ever heard. Downplaying the cancer all year, I finally realized that simply surviving was an award of immense merit. I'd been given the best gifts of all. Survival and appreciation.

Chapter 8

"Education's purpose is to replace an empty mind with an open one."

- Malcolm S. Forbes

"Students, teachers, parents, relatives, friends and distinguished guests, welcome." A few weeks after the awards night was the high school graduation. That day seemed like a final chapter in my battle against cancer. Here I was walking across yet another stage that marked the end of a childhood and the beginning of my adult journey. My black gown whistled as I strode into the gymnasium. I thought the event would carry more emotional weight, but it was hard to get excited as I itched my head beneath the polyester cap. The speakers spoke of individuality and creativity to a crowd of young people dressed exactly the same. However, as I sat daydreaming, I realized that with the grace of fate and things bigger than me, my health would remain and my new life could start without obstacles. Once I could get out of this gown, my life would truly begin.

After the ceremony, my family and friends joined me for a large celebration at our local VFW hall. Yet, my mother also billed it as an end of chemotherapy party, which was fine with me. Hundreds of friends and relatives arrived to congratulate me. Many of them expressed pride in the way that they felt I pulled through the illness with such a positive attitude. Was my outcome somehow helped by the way I never gave up hope? Did my optimism keep me from catching a cold or ameliorate the fatigue and stress? I don't know, but I know that it felt better than complaining for six months.

Most importantly, my family and close friends provided a level of support that sustained my health and heart. Without their constant reassurances, I never could have stayed so positive. Without their understanding, I couldn't have expressed intermittent frustration and anger. Without friends dropping by with a casserole, or doing the laundry, my parents couldn't focus on helping me to recover. Without their help watching and distracting my sister, I would have been even more obsessed with remaining stoic for her.

Finally, at the party I learned what my parents had gotten me as a graduation present. Since they'd spent so much money renting out the function hall and catering the event, they didn't have much to spend on an extravagant gift. Instead, my mother spent about four or five months before graduation collecting pictures from family and friends to put together an incredible photo album of my life. It was like game show, "This is your Life" in print. The book was complete with newspaper clippings from the day I was born through to graduation. It was truly a compilation of all my fondest memories. Though I teased them about wanting a car, it was the best present my parents could have given me. There were many pages left to fill in the book and my life as an adult was now beginning.

The end of the summer eventually rolled around and it was time to prepare for the entrance into college. I collected everything I needed for my freshmen year in college and left for my first taste of life at Dartmouth, my D.O.C. Trip. The letters D-O-C stand for the Dartmouth Outing Club. Every year before freshmen move into their rooms, they go away on various kinds of outing trips (hiking, biking, kayaking, etc.) to meet people before they arrive on campus. There were many new and wonderful people on my hiking trip, but there was one person in particular who made an immediate impact.

After hiking for four days, we arrived back at the main mountain lodge to take a bus back to campus. I was one of the last people to board for the ride home and only one seat remained in the back of the bus. I made my way back as my big bags hit everyone along the way. I wearily plopped myself down next to a short kid who looked as filthy and tired as I was. In what would turn out to be his natural tendency, he was talking and getting to know the people around him. After I got my belongings settled, the bus began to pull away. As the lodge disappeared behind us, I introduced myself.

"Hi, my name's Kyle Roderick," I said wearily.

"Hey, I'm Rex Morey, how ya doin? How was your trip? Where are you from?"

We continued to make small talk along with the rest of the group at the back of the bus. All the while, Rex dug into what looked like the most delicious Ben and Jerry's ice cream in the world. I didn't know what flavor it was and I didn't care. All of us had been in the woods for four days, eating couscous and trail mix. Rex's ice cream met the cardboard container in a silky, creamy embrace. The sweat on the outside of the ice cream container would have been enough to satisfy the hunger that overtook my stomach. My tummy was ready to charge me with homicide if I didn't appease it with something other than a grain or a nut. It wanted fat, sugar, grease – and Rex's velvety Ben and Jerry's Ice cream fit the bill perfectly.

He must have noticed me drooling all over myself staring at his ice cream. Without hesitation, Rex offered me the rest. I should have known then that this "short, filthy kid" was going to be a big part of my life here at school. His generosity was appreciated, and I hope he didn't regret his offer because I grasped the ice cream and devoured it before he could change his mind.

Shortly after my D.O.C. trip, I returned to Hanover, New Hampshire with my parents and little sister in tow. It was September, 1995 and the New Hampshire autumn was settling in. It was still warm and the leaves hadn't yet revealed the full brilliance of their colors. My family and I showed up after both of my roommates had arrived, so I was stuck with the last bed and desk. Ugh, how disappointing. These kids already chose the best stuff. Mom and Dad stayed to help me set up my room. We made my bed, hung posters, arranged my closet and set up the desk. I was overwhelmed with all of the new sights, sounds and smells of this fantastic place. Even though I got the last bed, the experience of independence was intoxicating. I was still as in love with this place as the first time I'd seen it.

Beep! Beep! Beep!

What the? What time is it? Where am I?

The following morning, my alarm clock rang to begin the first day of college classes. The fall term began to meet my high expectations quite immediately. My professors presented me with ideas and challenges I'd never imagined in my small town of Wareham. More importantly, I began to meet people that were so different from me that I had no choice but to learn.

Rex and I hit it off instantly. After he offered me that slice of heaven on the bus, I felt it would be wise to hang around with him. As social butterflies, we had an incredible time meandering around meeting so many of these new and diverse people. There were students from all over the country - all over the world. There were people from completely different social, economic, political, and religious backgrounds. I was amazed at all the incredible things and people that I was now surrounded with. I quickly realized that if I'd invest the energy, I could learn so much from these vastly different perspectives.

In contrast, I also attempted to maintain some semblance of a friendship with Heather. Most married couples are never forced to endure as traumatic an experience as cancer, yet we went through it as high school students. We had been through so much together. We had laughed so much together. We had cried so much together. It seemed that I almost felt indebted to her for sticking by me and being a shoulder to cry on through extremely turbulent waters. I had refused to see a counselor so Heather became my version of therapy. It was too difficult to let that go. Yet, here I was in a new place learning so many new things. She had no idea how quickly my mind was developing in Hanover. It's fair to say I was changing.

As I began to meet people at school, my relationship with Heather became more complex. We fought over "other people" and regular teenage issues. As many immature couples do, we bickered about little things. It was amazing how far my life had come from the days of chemotherapy and cancer. I was finally back to being a "normal" young adult and thought that it was a blessing. I thought that worrying about these silly normal things was where I wanted to be. What I know now is that being normal is not a blessing. What I know is that perhaps I hadn't learned the right lessons the first time.

I was back to worrying about little things - stressing about papers, worried about social status, being independent from my parents. In my desire to deny the true gravity of my battle with cancer, I had neglected to use it to alter my perception of life. This disease could have killed me and here I was worrying about girls.

Chapter 9

"In this life we will encounter hurts and trials that we will not be able to change; we are just going to have to allow them to change us."
- Ron Lee Davis

The whitewashed landscape of New Hampshire was stunning. The snow and ice covered the branches of the now bare trees, the panes of darkened windows, the hills surrounding Dartmouth College. Footprints in freshly fallen snow revealed the paths of students on their way to Sociology or Shakespeare. Frost on the windows clung to the corners of the glass almost as it did that fateful night in my parent's kitchen.

However, the arctic temperatures began to take their toll as the weeks progressed. One frigid early morning, I awoke to a terrible feeling.

Ugh, man I feel horrible. My throat hurts, my muscles ache and I'm hotter than hell. Crap, I think I have the flu!

As the day wore on, the lymph nodes in my necks began to swell as a natural response to the infection. I rested as often as possible and despite a low-grade fever, seemed to make a speedy recovery. Within a week or so I was feeling much better, but one lymph node on the right side of my neck remained curiously swollen. As the other lymph nodes shrank with my recuperation, the rogue node became more noticeable.

As each day passed I awoke and anxiously examined my neck in the mirror. Man, it's still there. Soon I was losing sleep and became increasingly irritable. The combination of stress, anxiousness, and lack of sleep drove me to near madness as I constructed every possible scenario in my mind. Each night I lay awake imagining reasons why this lymph node wouldn't disappear. This node represented a tangible reminder that I wasn't as healthy as I had wanted to believe. If it wasn't for my history of cancer, I probably wouldn't have worried about such a small thing. However, it signaled danger - extreme danger.

As the week passed, other people began to notice and ask me what was wrong with my neck. One day at lunch, I walked back to a table of friends with my fried chicken and string beans. A friend sitting a few tables away called over to me.

"Kyle! Come here," she said. "What's the matter with your neck?"

Her announcement in the crowded cafeteria publicized my most intimate fears. How did she see it from way back there? This thing must be huge. Something is definitely wrong. Eventually, I confessed my suspicions to my old therapist, Heather.

"I'm not sure what I'm going to do." I admitted uneasily.

"I mean, the end of the term is almost here. Maybe I can wait and make an appointment for myself when I get home. I'll get it taken care of then."

I'm not sure now how I figured I could hide it from my parents, especially my mother, but I just didn't want to worry them if I didn't have to.

They'd been through enough without involving them in what could turn out to be a false alarm. However, as I became increasingly distressed over the situation, Heather finally took it upon herself to tell my parents. At first I was livid, but eventually relieved that I wouldn't be the only one concerned about this. My mother called me and said she'd already lined up appointments in Boston for when I came home. We'd figure out whatever was causing this together. My experiences with cancer have taught me it is often more worrisome "not to know" and be in constant, agonizing anticipation than to just know what is actually happening. At least if I knew, I'd be able to react.

After finals at Dartmouth, I returned home. I was eager to deal with this lump in my neck. Home a few days, my mother, father and I went to an appointment at Children's hospital in Boston with Dr. Jones. He felt my neck, probed around a little, and then began to explain that he felt the only way to be sure that the lump was benign was to do a biopsy. To do this, he would have to cut my neck open and remove the lump while I was under general anesthesia.

However, by the time I met with Dr. Jones, the lump in my neck had begun to shrink. I interpreted this reduction within my paradigm of denial. I was through with this cancer business and if this lymph node had gone down, it must mean that it was simply an infection. Cancer cells only multiply unless some measure is taken to destroy them. Knowing that the lump was decreasing, I told my parents and the doctor that I didn't want to be cut open.

"Look, the lymph node has gone way down. If it was a tumor, it would have gotten bigger. That must mean that it was just the infection and I'll be fine," I half-shouted as I readied to stand and leave. "I'm not going to let anyone cut me open if it was just an infection."

Dr. Jones wouldn't have it. His harangue began.

"Kyle, you owe it to your future to have this over and done with. You have to know for sure. You owe it to yourself, your parents, and even me!" He rose from his stool and stood over me. "I have invested a lot of time into your illness now, and I'm not going to let you just blow it off because of some small operation! We can make a small incision, remove the lymph node and test it." His voice grew louder as I glanced at my parents. I couldn't believe his audacity but it scared me. I wondered why he was so insistent. "You HAVE to do this!" he finished.

My mother began to cry and practically pleaded with me to have the operation. What the heck is going on here? Can't they see that it's just an infection? I was completely taken aback by the reaction I got. I had expected everyone to feel the same way I did. I remained reluctant until my father, who was usually quiet and uncomfortable in a hospital setting, finally spoke.

"Kyle, maybe you should just get it over and done with," he suggested gently.

My father usually didn't speak up in this kind of situation. He never made a habit out of telling me what to do so I knew that his advice was fair. In the end, I was convinced to simply have the surgery, if as much to assuage my parents as to know the truth.

"Fine, Fine . . . When do you want me to come back to have the surgery?" I asked, begrudgingly.

"Tomorrow."

"TOMORROW?"

"Yes, I want you to come back tomorrow. It will be an outpatient surgery, and we should know the results in a week or so."

The next day, my parents and I drove an hour back to Boston during horrendous rush hour traffic. We got to Children's and parked. Every fiber of my being yearned to be somewhere else. I thought I was sure that this was all a big misunderstanding, but what if I was wrong? It seemed this illness was behind me, yet here I was worrying about it again. This was all supposed to be over by now.

We rode the elevator up to Dr. Jones' office and his nurses quickly readied me for the procedure. Dr. Jones made a small incision on the right side of my neck. The opening was a few inches above the inside corner of my collarbone. He removed the enlarged lymph node and sent it to pathologists to work on. They would surely get to the bottom of this situation. I just hoped The Chart wouldn't get any longer.

Please let this just be an infection.

I was allowed to go home later that afternoon with five or six stitches, and some butterfly bandages to keep the wound shut. Dr. Jones informed me that the scar would eventually blend into the natural wrinkles of my neck. There is still a small purple scar many people mistake for a hickey. You'd be amazed at how many people think I have a big hickey. It's pretty funny now. They are always so excited about the drama of it all, so sometimes I let them believe it.

After the surgery came another agonizing waiting game. My family resumed their normal activities as the days wore on. My sister was back in her dance classes, mom and dad were back at work. My spring break would have been like any other if it weren't for this fear itching at the back of my skull. I dove into work at a local restaurant and spent time with friends to distract myself. But deep down, I knew the pathology report could change my life all over again.

While we waited for the tests, I obeyed orders to stay close to home. No spring break trips for Kyle, they declared. My mother remained in constant touch with Dr. Jones' secretary regarding the test results. One week before I was scheduled to return to school, Dr. Jones' secretary called to inform my mother that most of the test results were back.

"Mrs. Roderick, most of the tests have come back from the pathology lab," the secretary began. "It looks as if he just had an infection after all! There are a few specialized DNA tests we are still waiting for, but I wanted to call and give you what good news I could."

My mother was overjoyed by the news. Her only son wouldn't be required to endure more rounds of chemotherapy. She would not lose him now. It was just an infection. On a calm spring Wednesday night, my mother invited my grandparents, aunts, uncles, and cousins to our house for ice cream, and a cake that read, "Hooray, it's just an infection!"

Of course, as a nineteen year old, I already thought my mom was probably the least cool parent on earth. Her outbreak of "hooray" justified my suspicions. It seemed my early reluctance to have the lymph node biopsy was justified as well. The secretary confirmed what I'd already believed. Yet, I was still uneasy about the rest of the tests, but I chalked it up to the anxiousness I had experienced all week. Maybe I'm still just all worked up. This really is great news. Thursday, I packed up my belongings and got ready to return to school on Monday. My mom suggested I pack so that I needn't worry about it over the weekend.

On Friday, I traveled from Wareham back to Boston for a scheduled gamma globulin treatment. These treatments are essentially antibodies to help supplement a weakened immune system. The bags of white goo were hung and dripped into my arm once a month since my first rounds of chemotherapy. In fact, I had grown fond of the hours each month I spent talking with the nurses at the Dartmouth College infirmary while I was at school. On this Friday, both my parents were busy so my Aunt Claire drove me to the hospital that the morning. I sat in a leather armchair watching TV for a few hours as the antibodies drip dropped down the plastic IV tubing into my arm. We drove home around 3pm.

When we pulled into the driveway, Aunt Claire shut off the car. That's weird, I thought. As I opened the door, she got out to walk me inside. This seemed out of the ordinary. I expected her to simply drop me off. She'd taken me to various appointments over the previous few years and rarely stopped to come in. Maybe she just wants to talk to mom about something. We both walked in the front door to the house. I saw my mother first. She appeared tremendously distraught, and my father was also home. I wonder what is wrong with her, and why is he home so early. As I glanced around with a puzzled look on my face, it all started to come together. Something serious was going down.

"Where's Dana?" I said with an exasperated tone.

"She's at a friend's house, come in and sit down please," my mother replied.

Immediately I sensed something was drastically wrong. Oh no. A closer look at my mother's face revealed told me she had been sobbing. Her nose and eyes are unnaturally red. In her hand was a tissue. My father's face didn't betray what he was probably thinking, but I noticed a distressed and distant look as he stared at the rug beneath him. He was kicking his toes into the ground like a child does when they do not want to hear what they are being told.

My first thoughts were something awful had happened to one of my grandparents. I had three living grandparents who are all elderly, and feared that perhaps one of them is sick, or worse.

My mother began, "Please sit down Kyle."

"What's the matter?" I continued with an angry tone that I didn't fully understand.

"Please sit."

"I don't want to sit down! What the hell is wrong?"

I felt angered at her quiet request to sit, not wanting bad news. There was a pause in the conversation. My mother's eyes fell to the floor. The tempo of my father's restless feet quickened on the rug.

"What's going on? Why won't you just tell me?"

"Kyle, the doctor called back today while you were at the hospital."

"Yeah, and… "

"Well, Kyle, he said that not all the tests had been in. [sniff] Remember there were a few tests that hadn't come back yet? Those tests came back today, and they show that your cancer has relapsed."

"What?"

"I'm so sorry, Kyle. I don't know what to say."

My mother began to sob again. My father sighed. Suddenly I couldn't breathe.

What emotions must accompany telling your nineteen year old son such terrible news? The parent-child relationship is clearly the strongest and most sensitive bond our culture knows. The hearts of my parents must have been writhing with pain having to tell their only son such terrible news. Pieces of my mother's heart escaped through her tears. She cried into a tissue hoping to stifle her sniffles. My father's foot kicks the floor with increasing pace. How horrific they must feel. If they could give anything in the world to take this pain away, they would. If they could take the cancer from their child and bear it themselves, surely they would. But the harsh reality is they cannot.

It's hard to fully explain the emotions that washed over me at that moment. I could not contemplate my cancer had survived. When I was first diagnosed with lymphoma, it forced me to examine my views of mortality and death. However, within this exploration of mortality, there remained a trace of invincibility that created a sense of hope and a stronger will to fight. I thought, this can't be right, there's no way I can die now. I won't let it happen! Sure, I had been diagnosed with cancer and people die from it, but I was deluded into believing that I would not become another statistic. It was a mild form of denial, but it helped me to stay positive. However, as my mother shares this news, I find out that my first fight was futile, meaningless.

This stuff is real. I seriously underestimated this cancer thing. I really might die.

This recurrence was immensely more disturbing and disheartening than the initial diagnosis. During this brief two-minute conversation with my parents, my life was again altered in ways I could never have imagined. The first time, I was shocked, angry and filled with disbelief. Now I am shocked, scared and filled with bewilderment.

I did not say anything, but finally heed my mother's advice to sit down. Nobody speaks for several minutes. There is just silence – and agony. I sit at the head of the kitchen table closest to where my mother is standing. My father is still leaning against the couch in the adjoining living room and my mother is standing a few feet from him in the kitchen. My aunt walks in behind me and cries, though not as loudly as my mother. I look at her and wonder why she has come inside. What I didn't know is that while we were at the hospital, my mother called and asked the secretary to bring my aunt to the phone. My aunt had known the whole time we were at the hospital.

As I sit down, Aunt Claire follows me and sits at the side of the table, taking my left hand into hers. I let out a long, deep, trembling sigh. It closely resembles the sigh my father gave when we received that first fateful phone call - a somber, sobering sigh. I don't know what else to do or say, so I try to breathe. I am absolutely shocked.

We had a party just two days ago didn't we? My clothes are all packed. I'm ready to return to school for the spring term! I'm already set to go back. They told us that it was just an infection.

This is ridiculous! How can they just change their minds like this?

None of these thoughts came out of my mouth. I knew from the way my mother said it, she'd probably already asked these, or at least similar questions. There was no way I could talk my way out of this. I continued to sit in the chair at the head of the table, completely stunned. Mom walked over and put her arms around me, still sobbing. My father's hand began slowly stroking my back up and down. They both tried to comfort me. Their efforts were appreciated, but sadly inadequate. Perhaps they already knew this, but there was nothing they could do. Nothing anyone could do right then. I think they were waiting for me to say something, or perhaps nobody knew what else to say. The uncomfortable silence, though overbearing and filled with anguish, was the only thing we knew to do at the moment.

A boiling stew of harsh emotions stirred in my head. Yet, one feeling emerged quickly above the rest. I felt strangely as though I'd just been slapped in the face. I had been so complacent, so content with my life. I felt like I'd forgotten everything I learned from my first experiences with cancer. Then I came out of remission. I was slapped in my face, sucker punched. It was almost as if I was being taught a lesson for not giving proper credence to the first battle with cancer.

Unfortunately, I hadn't been mature enough, or aware enough, to understand those lessons at the time. In high school, I had indeed grown from an angry, scared and stoic child into a self-confident and more focused young man. This was the first stage of the psychological and intellectual development arising from my disease. However, I hadn't allowed the experience to change my perspective on life and death. It had merely been an inconvenient obstacle – albeit a scary one. Nevertheless, I should have known better. I felt like my face was slapped as a kind of wake up call. It was a sign that I still had much to learn about the difference between living your life and being alive. Of course, I knew that fate didn't really work this way, but in a time like this, your mind grasps on to anything that seems to make more sense of the situation.

As we sat at the kitchen table, I was too shocked for it to sink in. Tears would not roll yet. I was not rational. My thoughts were barely coherent. It was almost as if I didn't believe my mother's words.

Like bits of artificial snow in a cheap glass snow-globe, my emotions cover my thoughts. The small plastic city can, at first, be seen through tiny flakes. However, rational thoughts are becoming harder to form through the building emotions. Slowly the snow descends upon the city in an unrelenting storm that collects on every surface. My emotions create a blanket of anger, of fear, of disbelief over every tangible idea that I can still form.

Eventually the snow would swirl away from the tiny plastic buildings. Someone bumped the table, shook the globe. The landscape and city were visible again. Realizations began to surface, semblances of reality were uncovered and reappeared. Instead of shock, disbelief and fear (all intangible), I began to wonder what this remission would actually mean to me. I pondered what would happen in the months ahead, and more specifically, my chances of survival.

What kinds of chemotherapy will I need to endure? Can I go back to school? Can I really live through this all over again? Can I do this?

I became more overwhelmed by the news and had to leave the room. I needed to be by myself for a while. Cancer is a hard disease to deal with. It felt like I had been branded and dispatched to an island by myself. Now I was inside the cheap glass snow-globe. I was walking down an abandoned alley in the plastic city. No one was around, no one could find me. The snow, now disturbed, made the city cold and unbearably uninviting. There was nothing that my nearest family or closest friends could do or say to comfort me. I was faced with my own mortality again and there was no one who could share these feelings with me. Perhaps they could empathize. Maybe they could feel pity, want to help, wish to comfort, but there's no way they could share my feelings. I felt so alone. I was in a cheap glass snow-globe, walking down an abandoned alley at two in the morning.

As I walked down the hallway to retreat my bedroom, I began to cry. The only saving grace of an abandoned alley is that you can feel however you damn well want to feel. It got tiring trying to be indifferent for everyone else. The charade could end. Here I could cry. I cried for myself. I cried for my loss of freedom. I cried for my loss of innocence. I cried for my family and their pain. I cried because I was alone. I cried because I was afraid to die.

Chapter 10

"Crisis forces our attention on the disorder in our thinking and can save us just as we teeter on the brink of an even greater disaster."
- David McNally

    The following morning the oncologists at Dana-Farber broke the hard news to me. The words were cold and blunt. "It would be impossible for you to go back to school right now. We are looking at the possibilities of high dose chemotherapy, but we haven't found the right protocol for treatment yet. The only thing we can tell you is that you can't go back to Dartmouth for the spring term. I'm sorry."

    Time passed in a whirlwind of fleeting moments of terror and semi-consciousness. Within a week, I was collecting my belongings from Dartmouth. Allowed to return for a few days to tie up loose ends, I packed up my things, and returned home. Leaving school was a tremendously difficult experience. My love for Dartmouth and the number of friends I made there had grown rapidly in the first six months. I'd always been a social butterfly and in the melting pot of adolescence surrounding my freshman year at college, I'd blossomed. Yet, as I started packing up my belongings, friendships and autonomy, it was extremely painful. I had finally been afforded the opportunity to separate myself from my parents and the hospital. See, that was the thing. I had been normal again for a while. I'd known independence not only from my parents, but more importantly, from health issues.

Now I was being thrust back into the overprotective environment from which I wanted to escape. It had taken so long to begin to grow and mature as my own person. Yet, this damn cancer was back and ripping that carpet of freedom from beneath me. I just wanted to have a normal life.

So I resentfully returned to Dartmouth College, choked back tearful good-byes and meekly attempted to explain the situation to my friends. The close ones knew the full story. They'd prayed and hoped with my family while we waited for those pathology tests. They knew about the tacky cake, they knew it had all been a lie. They were as saddened and disappointed as the rest of my family.

The rest of my friends saw a healthy-looking boy moving his things out of his room. They were unprepared for the news that I was leaving because I had cancer. I was nervous about how they'd react. I was nervous as I remembered the mixed results I saw in high school. The looks on their faces illustrated their confusion, their shock. Nobody closed up, or shied away from discussion, but it was still hard.

I continued to pack my belongings and tried to resolve issues on campus until my father arrived to bring me home. The close ones were there again. They cried as they helped me load my things into my father's van. I felt cheated as we slowly pulled away. Peering out the side window,

I saw the dark green oak doors of the dormitories getting smaller in the mirror as we drove off. My life had been turned upside down again. And I had already fought this battle goddammit!

Back at home, things got worse. My family and I began the long process of simultaneously developing a medical treatment plan and relearning how to peacefully navigate the family dynamics. Just because I had cancer didn't mean all was tranquil and free of conflict. If anything, combining a collectively heightened emotional state with a twelve-year-old and an angry college freshman set the stage for World War Three.

The first problem was a different sleeping pattern. The sleeping habits of two forty-year olds, a twelve-year-old, and a nineteen-year-old college freshmen are drastically different. My sister was always in bed first, and then the house would quiet down. Eventually my parents retired. After a few hours watching television or reading, I would go to my bedroom and call friends who were still away at college. None of them were in their rooms before eleven so I had to call late at night. Our house is relatively small so almost every night my mother woke up and yelled at me for being on the phone so late. To resolve some of this tension, we moved my bedroom downstairs to the basement, and I hunkered down in this battle trench and prepared for a long war.

Immediately following my return from Dartmouth, the intense medical procedures began. We began meeting regularly with physicians at the Dana-Farber Cancer Institute to determine the best course of action. Unfortunately, my original oncologist, Dr. Shimbara, had left on maternity leave. Another oncologist took her place, Dr. Greg Kernan.

Time continued to pass in a whirlwind of meetings and tests. Dr. Kernan wanted to obtain a baseline of my body functions. He wanted to see what types of treatment my body could endure and these tests would also allow him to compare any losses post-treatment. During this time, I traveled back and forth between the city and Wareham. An ear test here, and eye test there, hearing test, there a test, everywhere a test, test. I felt like a pincushion. Of the many pokes and prods, the most important investigation centered on my immunological status.

Immunologists at Boston's Children's Hospital believed that my extreme reaction to the Epstein Barre virus was caused by X-linked Lymphoproliferative Syndrome (XLP) or Duncan's disease. XLP is an extremely rare, primarily inherited, immunodeficiency disorder characterized by a defective immune system response to infection with the Epstein-Barr virus. In most cases, individuals experience an onset of symptoms anytime from approximately six months to ten years of age. Some studies suggest that people with XLP rarely live past forty years of age. This might explain why my reaction to the virus during high school had been so dramatic.

Mononucleosis (mono), is common among the general population and usually causes no long-lasting effects. Unfortunately, in individuals with

XLP, exposure to the virus can result in severe, life-threatening disease. Such a significant infection can also cause increased susceptibility to other viruses and malignancies of certain types of lymphoid tissue. It might even present at lymphoma.

It was during these rounds of discussions that the team of doctors from Dana-Farber first broached the subject of bone marrow transplantation.

"Mr. and Mrs. Roderick, Kyle, we believe the only way we can offer you a chance of a cure is to have you go through a bone marrow transplant. It is very risky given your underlying immune system, but this cancer came back so quickly . . . We feel that an autologous transplant is our only option"

"What the hell is a bone marrow transplant?" I shot off angrily.

Dr. Kernan began to explain the procedure. Bone marrow is the soft spongy tissue inside bones. This tissue creates red blood cells to carry oxygen, white blood cells to fight infection and platelets to control clotting of the blood. During an autologous transplant, a physician removes a small amount of a patient's own bone marrow, administers high doses of chemotherapy and/or radiation to kill cancerous cells, and rescues the patient with their own marrow after the treatment is complete. This procedure is more common than an allogeneic transplant, which requires a bone marrow donor. Autologous transplants generally lead to fewer complications because the marrow is from the patient's own body. This eliminates the possibility of graft rejections and graft-versus-host disease, but there are still many dangers. These can be one of the most devastating complications from a transplant. In a solid organ transplant, the body can reject the donated organ. With bone marrow, the new blood can actually reject the body resulting in graft-versus-host-disease or GVHD.

As Dr. Kernan explained the gravity of bone marrow transplantation and the rationale for this drastic approach to treatment, my heart sank back into the cesspool of hopelessness and despair that I'd experienced when my mother first told me that the cancer had come back. There would be no short hospital stays this time. The doctors were scouring the literature, trying to find options, but thus far, transplantation with the only path. Something inside me knew that any other known options would be futile, it would come down to a decision to transplant or not transplant.

In the interim, the team decided that I should go through a three-day regimen of inpatient high dose chemotherapy. This would contain the present cancer cells and buy us some time until we reached a final decision. They scheduled the inpatient stay for a few weeks away back at Children's Hospital. We left Dana-Farber with less hope than with which we entered. The car ride home was eerily silent as my parents and I separately wrestled with our own emotions.

During these weeks, my mother and I went to the various hospitals where I'd been treated, to collect my medical records. This proved to be a rather harrowing adventure. As we went from hospital to hospital, we became increasingly frustrated with the widespread disorganization and bureaucratic roadblocks. Oftentimes the records offices were unable to locate important records. This phenomenon was not confined to just one hospital, it appeared to be citywide.

At one point, we went to the medical records office in the basement of Children's Hospital to obtain laboratory results they had previously been unable to find. After a long explanation to the secretaries about what we were looking for and its importance, they finally found what they said were the results of my tests. As my mother and I boarded the elevator to leave, I opened the manila envelope to discover the results of someone else's tests. Even in the highly litigious society we live in, mistakes happen with unnerving frequency in our healthcare system. We brought the stranger's results back to the office – they were never able to find mine.

Eventually we compiled all the documents we could, packed them in a large cardboard box, and sent them to the country's leading expert on XLP, Dr. Armitage at the University of Nebraska Medical Center. Dr. Armitage was charged to look over all of the pertinent medical information and provide an opinion on a course of treatment. If anyone in the country could decide the best outcome for my situation, it would likely be this physician.

The third opinion we sought was from the New England Medical Center (NEMC, now Tufts Medical Center) in Boston. My mother was determined to get as much information as possible before she allowed me to decide my future. As we sat in the freshly painted waiting room of the hematology/oncology division of NEMC, I felt strangely at ease. The pine paneled walls, carpeted floors and large windows presented a sense of bucolic easiness and respectability. I felt more like a person in that place – less a case study. It's amazing what a little area rug and some sunshine can do for the human spirit.

I also remember meeting Dr. David Schenkein for the first time. Dr. Schenkein strode briskly into the exam room with an air of confidence tempered by humility. He was a relatively young man in his early forties. I immediately sensed a balance of professionalism and humor. Perhaps it was the way he shook my hand, but something in him expressed to me that this man might be a good leader for my team of doctors.

I digress here to suggest that what I offer about my feelings for Dr. Schenkein are not merely metaphorical. In my most humble opinion, I am under the impression that we, as humans, communicate more comprehensively than with mere words. There are, of course, non-verbal cues that we share with each other.

However, I am referring to a much subtler connection. Take for instance the honeybee. We all know that with just a few molecules of the correct pheromone emitted by the queen, every other bee in the hive knows exactly what she wants. Plants can even signal each other to warn the others of an impending virus. As the most intelligent creatures on the planet, we may overlook the more delicate ways in which we interact. The next time you walk into a room and can "feel the tension," maybe there is more truth to the statement than you realize.

This point should not be lost on patients who are evaluating their health care providers. If you feel less than comfortable with a particular provider, you must appreciate that you are your own best advocate. It does not mean that this particular provider is a bad person, or even a bad physician. It simply means that something between the two people in the interaction is not harmonious. That disjunction may only hurt your healthcare and chances of a successful outcome in the end. To write off your instincts as impractical or inconsequential may be doing a disservice to you and your health.

This is all to say that the immediate sense of wellbeing I felt around Dr. Schenkein gave me the first glimmer of hope I'd felt in weeks. Who knows what kinds of positive neurotransmitters I experienced as a result of this sense of hope. Dr. Schenkein read the chart of his new patient thoroughly and either felt positively about my treatment or was simply a positive thinker. Regardless, he lent me a measure of his optimism. My mother, father, and I spent the first visit reviewing each aspect of my case and venting slightly about the lack of direction we'd seen. We left with his assurance that he'd work diligently to put together a comprehensive treatment regimen. My family and I now knew that we had three sets of experts trying to figure out the best way to cure my cancer.

In less than a week, Dr. Schenkein called us back to New England Medical Center. He had something to discuss. He said he would prefer to meet in person. My mother and I drove back to Boston, checked in, and waited for the news. Hopefully, we'd hear something more definitive.

Dr. Schenkein entered the room with the same confident manner as before. He first expressed that his team and Dana-Farber had agreed on a few points. Neither team was convinced with the XLP diagnosis I received at Children's Hospital. They agreed that Severe Combined Immunodeficiency (SCIDs) was a more likely candidate for my problems. SCIDs is a disease in which there is a defect in both the T-lymphocyte and B-lymphocyte systems causing a larger susceptibility to infections and occurs in approximately 1 in 75,000 births. Severe Combined Immunodeficiency Disease is generally considered the most serious of the primary immunodeficiency diseases because all adaptive immune functions are absent. Therefore, SCIDs is actually more devastating than XLP in that there is susceptibility to more organisms than just the Epstein-Barre virus. The condition is fatal unless transplants of the defective tissue or enzyme replacement can reconstruct the immune system.

This fact, while obviously bad news, meant little more than a different set of letters to me until Dr. Schenkein continued. His usually lighthearted demeanor quietly morphed into something more somber.

"Kyle and Mrs. Roderick," He began with a straight face.

"While I agree with Dana-Farber's assessment of the severity of the immune deficiency, something else came to my attention. The physicians at Dana-Farber are leaning toward an autologous bone marrow transplant."

"Yes, we know. So what?" I chimed in apprehensively.

"In my opinion, an autologous transplant would leave Kyle with the same underlying immune deficiency that may have started this mess. We feel that for him to have any hope for a cure for this lymphoma, Kyle needs an allogeneic transplant."

"That seems to make sense, I can't believe no one had thought of that," I agreed.

"Well, Dana-Farber may have thought of it. The immune deficiency itself may make any transplant difficult, especially an allogeneic transplant. The other problem is that you'd need a donor, a bone marrow donor. However, while we ultimately feel this is really the best option for long term survival, I think we need a better understanding of your immune system – and that will take time. We'd suggest you wait and let's run some more tests."

Hell, long term survival certainly seemed like a good goal to aim for. When Dr. Schenkein spoke to me, I viewed the lymphoma as either curable or incurable, life or death. Only very recently has cancer begun to be viewed and treated as a long-term chronic illness – much like diabetes, or heart failure. An autologous transplant meant fewer risks to my body, but I'd survive with the same weakened immune system. An allogeneic transplant would present more danger; however I'd be buying a new car, not simply changing the tires. So why wait? I wanted it over with. Screw this "more tests" crap.

Chapter 11

After weeks of consideration, the final verdicts were in. The experts suggested two different courses of action. The Dana-Farber Cancer Institute informed us that the best chance for a cure and long-term survival would come from an autologous bone marrow transplant - as soon as possible. Dr. Schenkein and his colleagues decided that the most prudent course of action would be to gain a better understanding of my immune functions before proceeding with any forms of treatment as serious as a transplant.

Between 1988 and 1990, approximately 12,000 allogeneic bone marrow transplants (BMTs) were performed worldwide, according to data compiled by the International Bone Marrow Transplant Registry. Only ten percent of these transplants were performed on patients with lymphoma. Typically, patients with Hodgkin's disease and non-Hodgkin's lymphomas who cannot be cured with conventional chemotherapy undergo an autologous bone marrow transplant rather than an allogeneic transplant. However, with my underlying immune deficiency, Dr. Schenkein felt that if a transplant was warranted after careful consideration, they would prefer an allogeneic transplant. The long-term survival rate following an allogeneic BMT is twenty percent, compared to zero to five percent with standard chemotherapy.

Everyone agreed I should go ahead with the three days of high dose chemotherapy at Children's Hospital in the meantime. I would remain under the care of Dana-Faber Cancer Institute. To my knowledge, Dr. Armitage hadn't contacted us yet. I wondered what was taking so long. Why hadn't he weighed in?

My family and I sequestered ourselves to begin deliberating on a final decision. My parents shouldered the difficult task of explaining to their teenage son that the decision ultimately rested in his hands. They sat me down one evening as I arrived home for dinner after a rare day of normalcy with my friends.

"Kyle, we need to talk," my mother said as I walked in the door and set down the keys.

"Yeah, sure. What's up?" I said.

My parents were sitting around the kitchen table again and an uncomfortable aura of trepidation hung in the air. I was beginning to hate that damn table. Their faces seemed to have grown much older in the last few months. I'd not noticed it before, but now I saw clearly the evidence of their own sleepless nights. Their son was facing a devastatingly difficult battle against cancer and his chances of survival teetered dangerously close to the slim side of things. I've no doubt they wanted nothing more than to steal him away from everything and hold on with all their collective might. Yet, they somehow found the courage to let him grow up.

"Kyle, you know we love you very much right?" my mother continued.

"Yeah, ma. Of course I do. Why?"

"Your father and I have been talking and we need to tell you something. We're just as afraid as you are about what is going to happen. The thing is – well, the thing is that you're an adult now. You're nineteen, and that means you're an adult."

"I know, ma, that's what I've been trying to tell you for years," I interjected with an uncomfortable smirk.

"Kyle, this decision is going to be up to you. We'll help you as much as we can, but the final decision will be yours."

It was all up to me. There was no consensus. Medicine had revealed itself to me as an amorphous ball of scientific jelly. There were defined principles that governed many diagnoses, but many more diseases seemed like jelly filled best-guess messes. My case was full of jelly and my parents were leaving the task up to me. From here on out, I would call the shots based on whatever information the physicians were able to provide.

My mind again raged with conflicting, contemptuous emotions. I loved my parents. I hated my parents. I hated my body. I wanted to live. I wanted it all to be over. I wanted it to be over in the right way. I wanted to be normal. I knew, in no uncertain terms, I'd never be normal again. It would be hard to explain all the feelings I had during this time, but a few excerpts from my journal may shed insight into a confused and anguished mind:

April 4, 1996

Went to Boston today, for Pre-op at Children's, and then over to Dana-Farber to obtain some records, then off to New England Medical Center for a second opinion. The doctor (Dr. Schenkein) seemed very nice and gave us more statistics than Dana-Farber did. But that really doesn't tell me anything. It would just be nice to know a definitive answer. I mean, I'm ready to "fight the fight" as mom would say, but it makes it so much harder when no one is saying, "yeah, this is what you have, these are your options, this option is the best one statistically." I mean really . . . plain and simple right? Unfortunately not.

My mental health is still relatively intact. I seem to be doing much better than anyone else, it's just that I seem to be getting something for nothing. My father told me, "You never get something for nothing in this world." Well, it appears this is an exception. What do I get for all of this? Do I get people's respect? No. I already had that - otherwise so many people wouldn't be worried. Does it build character? As far as I can tell, I already have a fairly good character. So why all this new stuff?

I couldn't figure it all out. I don't think I was meant to. It's just hard trying to keep everything balanced and in perspective when the rug is pulled from underneath you so damn rapidly. I read a quote today that was interesting . . . "people need to remember, every case is terminal. It just depends on how long you last" or something like that. I mean, yeah sure, I know we're all going to keel over someday, but I'd like to get my full ride. I don't want to get off a few exits early. I want to live a full and NORMAL life.

April 8, 1996

Well, this wonderful little story takes yet another dramatic and eventful twist. My second opinion was due to arrive. My mother and I waited for most of the day for Dr. Schenkein to call. All the while, the phone rang incessantly with concerned people wondering if he had called yet. The only problem was that every time the phone rang, mom jumped hoping it was him. Dr. Schenkein eventually called in the middle of the afternoon, and his answer:

"We feel it would be in Kyle's best interest to wait awhile. We don't know what's up with his immune system, and we should figure that out before we jump into a bone marrow transplant . . . We also feel that a bone marrow donor would be better than getting his own back."

Why all the drama? I just wanted to get this started and get on with my life. So many things are changing and will continue to change. Things as small as Heather's prom. She's all upset, because she doesn't know what to do. Either way we both lose; if I tell her I'd be uncomfortable with her going, then I'd feel bad that I asked her to miss her senior prom. If I tell her to go, then I'll be pissed off and wondering what she's doing and who she's with. She'll be mad if she can't go and not have fun if she does go. It all seems so trivial, especially in the face of such a serious disease, but it's these small "normal" things that matter now.

Eventually, it was time to get on with the treatment. On Wednesday April 10, 1996 I checked into Children's Hospital in Boston for the three day treatment the doctors had agreed upon. I went through the nurse's tests, weighed in and they escorted my parents and me up to the pre-operation room where I changed. After what seemed like eternity, a team of doctors entered the pre-op waiting room.

The doctors were preparing me for a central line or Hickman catheter. A central line is an intravenous line that winds its way directly into a person's chest. The IV enters a major vein in the chest or thigh or stomach. Once implanted it allows the nurses to draw blood or give injections without constantly pricking my arms and hands for a vein. My catheter was going to be implanted in my chest, wind through my shoulder and into a vein near my heart. As the doctors explained the procedure and risks to me, they mentioned that rarely a needle could puncture the patient's lung. If the needle accidentally penetrates the lung, the patient could be in serious danger.

The head surgeon, whose son happened to be a classmate at Dartmouth, assured me that this was extremely uncommon and boasted that he'd never punctured a lung before. I signed the appropriate papers and was given what he called the "feel good juice" - a medicine to calm me ready me for the anesthesia. I drifted off to some other place with a smile on my face.

When I awoke, I had a brand new white rubber hose protruding ten inches from my chest. The doctor's brought in an x-ray machine to make sure the hose had found the correct vein and that my lung wasn't punctured during the procedure. Everything checked out. Like a snake's tongue the hose dangled from my left pectoral muscle and slithered all the way down to my thigh. It looked horrific and my chest was stained orange from the betadine used as an antiseptic prior to surgery. The white gauze and clear plastic bandage around the hole in my chest made me feel extremely vulnerable. This attachment was not only foreign, it also led to an ignoble new opening in my body. The hole in my chest sat squarely above my heart and no amount of gauze or clear plastic bandage could remove the deep penetrating feeling of this literal new entrance to my heart.

Whether lucky or unlucky, this was all a precursor to the real deal. The oncology team decided to delay the chemotherapy for a day or two because they hadn't finished all the tests they wanted. On Thursday morning, a male and female nurse led me downstairs for a lumbar puncture (spinal tap). They wanted to be sure I had no cancer cells in my central nervous system.

As they wheeled me to the operating room, I began chatting with the male nurse.

"So what's the deal with this 'lumbar puncture'?" I ventured.

"Ah, it's a procedure to draw spinal fluid from your lower back. It helps the doctors determine if there are cancer cells in the central nervous system," he replied coolly.

"Huh," I replied, trying to mirror his calmness. "So does it hurt?"

"Kid, I can't lie to you, it hurts, but I'd guess you've been through many tests already. You can even be sedated for this test, it's up to you."

"Wait, sedated? Will I still feel the pain? What is the sedation supposed to do?" I asked in rapid fire succession.

"Well, it mostly relaxes you. It'll also make you forget what happened," he answered matter-of-factly.

"Wait, it will relax me and make me forget it, but does it do anything for the pain?"

"Well, no. But it will make you forget it."

His answer surprised me. I paused for a moment as I pondered his response. "Make me forget? No way, I'd rather just be there. I want to be awake for this."

The nurse guided me into the tiny procedure room at the end of a long hallway. In front of me stood a physician, a resident and a chrome table with several very long needles. The physician kindly asked me to lie down on the vinyl table and curl into a fetal position. He began explaining to the resident the proper way to perform a lumbar puncture. As a teaching hospital, the residents at Children's learn by doing basic procedures under the guidance of their attending physician. I was one of the lessons today.

The resident was clearly uneasy as he watched me lie down. In this hospital, I'd have likely been one of the oldest patients he'd seen. He lifted the needle and placed the sharp metal tip against the skin of my back. The physician showed him how to feel for the soft area between the vertebrae and when he was comfortable he attempted to guide the needle into my spinal cavity.

With no medication to ease the piercing pain, I was aware of every inch of that needle as it tore through my skin and muscle. Within seconds I could sense that something was wrong. The resident was unable to guide the tip of the needle home. Both nurses held my hands and I felt their empathy. My brow quickly filled with the sweat of intense pain and after several attempts, the physician finally spared me and took over. He withdrew a small amount of spinal fluid and finally removed the needle.

On our way back up to my room, the male nurse told me that I was the first person he had ever seen experience the spinal tap without sedation. He sounded at once amazed and confused. Why would a kid decide not to opt for medication?

I guess it was a control issue. I was on an emotional roller coaster, a ride with no control. Ninety percent of what happens to me is either predetermined or is a matter of happenstance. The more serious my condition became, the more power I lost. While objecting to the medication seemed like a trivial act of boldness to the nurse, it was everything to me. I clung to that defiance with everything I could because it was a decision – simply a decision. It didn't matter whether it was correct or not, it was a choice that only I could make. That retained what small bit of power I'd otherwise have lost.

After that conversation with the nurse, I realized it had become a pattern. The necessity to assert control over my situation overrode the logic of accepting as many mind-numbing drugs as possible. I'd long ago rationalized the value of control over pain as a tool in my arsenal of coping mechanisms. By rejecting the sedation, I proved to the world (or perhaps only myself) that I was strong and not helpless. As I recounted each test, each procedure, I'd always found ways to exert some level of control.

This was counter to my usual persona. Normally I was a "roll with the punches" kind of guy, but this disease had changed that. I wanted to be involved in the discussions, I wanted to refuse sedation. Something deeper than my consciousness yearned to exercise free will in an otherwise powerless situation.

On Friday, the chemotherapy commenced. It was around seven o'clock when the doctor first arrived to start the procedure. My agitation grew instantly as the physician took my vital signs and checked my chart. Something was wrong. I hadn't expected them to start before my father arrived and I didn't have a copy of the dosing reports. I'd requested my own copy so I'd be sure I was receiving the proper amounts of each drug. I'd lost a tremendous amount of trust in many healthcare providers. Perhaps this was a coping mechanism to retain a sense of control. Perhaps it was because they failed to cure the cancer the first time. In either case, I was extremely anxious about these higher doses of chemotherapy. In fact, a newspaper article that month detailed a story of a man who was given the wrong dose of chemotherapy and died. Stories like this, however uncommon, make me a little nervous.

Unfortunately, my mother had inadvertently taken the dosage report home with her. As soon as the room was clear, I called her in a hysterical fit. I told her that if I died it would be all her fault. My father had not arrived at the hospital yet, so I lay in the darkened hospital room all alone when the nurses came to hang the bags of poison. I'm sure it was due to sleep deprivation, the medications and stress, but as I recall it now, I can't imagine how those words must have torn at my mother's heart as she sat at home, a full hour away, knowing that her son was so upset to say something so hurtful.

My father showed up soon enough, however, and was able to calm me down. We settled in to watch a movie we had borrowed from the hospital library. "The River Wild" with Meryl Streep and Kevin Bacon. The movie is about a family that goes white water rafting and gets kidnapped by bank robbers. We sat quietly watching the film for about twenty minutes -the action had barely started, when all of a sudden, my stomach felt as if it was white water rafting with Meryl Streep. I began to feel extremely nauseous. Chemotherapy affects everyone differently and I'd handled the first rounds with little complaint. Yet, this higher dose and different chemicals affected me immediately. In a matter of minutes, my stomach became queasy and my mouth began to water. I tasted metal. I quietly asked my father for a bucket and as soon as he handed it to me I filled it with vomit.

The reaction was so strong that I bolted upright in my bed, and for the first time since I can remember, I began to cry in front of my father. The tears somehow began to purge me of the anxiety welling up inside. While everything was coming out, something else was happening. The anger, the fear, the bewilderment was collecting in my tears and I realized it was okay to cry right then. I felt the emotions draining from my eyes (and leaping from my stomach) It was uncomfortable at first to cry in front of my father, but it was the first time I'd felt relieved in weeks.

I had already been through this chemotherapy nonsense during high school, and here it was, all over again. I had tried to be stoic. I had tried to keep it all inside. I had tried to protect everyone around me from the pain and frustration I felt. However, this sudden materialization of my illness was overwhelming and the pain escaped my eyes in front of the one person I'd wanted most to be brave for. I remember exactly what I said to him that night.

"Dad, I just don't want to do this again."

He brought me a cool facecloth and for the first time throughout this whole ordeal, he expressed his emotions to me. I'm not sure now if he cried or not, but I know he was close because I could hear it in his voice. He grew up in a family that has a tenderness that is always there but not always obvious.

"Kyle, you're going to be alright. It may not be easy, but we've made it through this before, we can do it again if we have to."

He rose from his chair and sat next to me on the bed. He placed his large arms around me and held me there on my hospital bed. My dad looked at me with eyes full of pain and told me that we'd get through this together. He hugged his son and stroked my back, trying his best to ease my discomfort.

I don't think he knew it then, but that reassurance was the best that he (or anyone) could have done. I'm sure he was searching for ways to help. He always attempted to find something to do, some way to help me fight. But when those vile chemicals pumped through my bloodstream, the only thing he could do in that moment was hold me and tell me we would all be okay, we'd stick together. I finally realized I wasn't the only one fighting this ordeal. The cancer wasn't just threatening me, the patient - this was a family affair.

As the initial effects of the chemotherapy wore off, I settled into bed and tried to sleep. The sterile smell of the hospital sheets wafted around me, and each breath stirred the nausea. My father was asleep within minutes of the movie's end. My night had just begun. The lights in the hospital hallway dimmed to signal the end of the night and a shift change.

I lay in the bed wondering what would happen next. Familiar notions of uncertainty and fear began to brim and boil to the surface of my imagination. I nodded off to nightmares of death and tragedy that startled me into what seemed like an endless cycle of tossing and turning. As the night wore on, I became increasingly aware of a pain directly above my heart. For all I knew, it was simply my heart breaking as I began the process of chemotherapy all over again.

On Saturday morning I awoke to a throbbing pain in my chest. I complained briefly to the morning nurses about breathing difficulties, but tried to fight through it and was reluctant to admit that I was in terrible pain. I assumed it was a side effect of the insertion of this long tube in my chest. Jesus, this thing is killing me. I can barely breathe. I won't say anything – no, I just want to do my time and get the hell out of here.

My mother arrived early in the morning and immediately insisted that something was wrong with my breathing. Somehow she knew, she just knew. She complained all day as each resident that cycled through blew her off. As the hours wore on, the pain intensified. I tried to rationalize it, I wanted everything to go smoothly. She wouldn't leave until the doctors examined me thoroughly. After an hour of pleading with the evening shift, the doctors took another chest x-ray. It revealed that I had a collapsed left lung! It would require a chest tube.

My friend Rex, my cousin David, my sister Dana and a friend's mother had arrived over the course of the day and they stuck around as a mother fought for her son. It was late and we were all very tired. Graciously they all decided to spend the night in a Boston hotel to support my mother while she accompanied me into late-night surgery.

The chest surgery was the worst experience to date. I refused the wheelchair and walked through the hospital to the operating room. The room was extremely small and designed for relatively minor operations like a chest tube. The walls were covered with buttons, knobs and hoses. As residents and interns began to crowd the room, I felt like an animal on display. In a teaching hospital like Children's, there always seemed to be more people around than necessary.

The surgeon introduced a small dose of morphine and codeine into the tube in my chest. He then injected the left side of my chest with an anesthetic. Within seconds, his shiny steel scalpel pierced my skin and cut a hole in the cartilage between my ribs. The residents ooh'd and aah'd as they watched him make a hole in my rib cage. He inserted a tube into this new wound to relieve the pressure building outside my lungs. The tube was connected to a pump, which interrupted my natural breathing. My gasping breaths made me feel as though I was drowning and I was getting very frightened. Initially, Mom stood stolidly by my side.

"Mom, (gasp) . . . I feel like (gasp) . . . I'm drowning (gasp)."

My mother began to cry, quietly at first. "Just picture yourself at the beach, Kyle. Think of somewhere nice. Think of yourself lying on the beach somewhere other than here."

Surely, she missed the irony in that moment. She stood helpless as physicians dug scalpels into my ribcage. As her crying rapidly declined into uncontrollable sobbing that came from somewhere deep within her, she was asked to leave the room.

When the operation was complete there was a plastic tube protruding from two ribs on my left side. The tube was connected to a suction pump that slowly sucked air and fluid out of my chest cavity. The reduction in pressure would allow my lung to heal and re-expand to its normal size. When the time came to return to my room, I wasn't foolish enough to refuse the wheelchair this time.

A nurse wheeled me back through a maze of linoleum hallways. We continued through the labyrinth of fluorescent white and magical doors that opened without instruction. The hallways all looked the same and the morphine rendered the intelligent opening doors comical. We were traveling in circles for all I knew. It was if I was in another world.

Yet, the unmistakable aroma of a hospital permeated the walls and floors and I knew exactly where I'd end up. Dear God, that smell. The whiff of plastic IV tubing mingled awkwardly with sterilized metal instruments. Then the strong odor of antiseptic and detergent overpowered everything. The smells and hideous lighting had a way of dulling the senses and making me feel less than human. This place was not a place of comfort or relief. There was healing here, but it was a cold healing.

The suction pump slowly released the pressure as my lung healed and a morphine drip continued into Sunday. The morphine was to help ease the pain of a deflated lung and the tube roughly shoved into the cartilage between my ribs. It reset every few minutes, and administered a dose of narcotics that took me away to somewhere that was much better than the hospital bed.

While I was on the morphine pump, I only partially recall the faces of my visitors, and don't remember any conversations. Bits and pieces have returned, but most of my experience is wrapped in a cloud of semi-consciousness. Yet, there was one incident I do remember clearly. It was late afternoon and the day had already been long and wearing. I was in such agonizing pain over the course of the day that the doctors gave me various drugs to relax.

When they tried a new muscle relaxant, Trilafon (perphanazine), something terrible happened. All of a sudden, the muscles in my back began to constrict uncontrollably. My head was wrenched back and my shoulder blades clasped together. My elbows strained to touch behind my back and my feet slowly moved behind me towards my rear end. I was experiencing an acute dystonic reaction – prolonged muscle contractions that can cause twisting and repetitive movements or abnormal posture. While not painful, it was terribly frightening.

My good friend Bear sat in a chair next to my bed reading his college math book. He'd been coming by the hospital almost every day after class just to sit and relieve my mother for a few hours. As he focused on his book, he hadn't noticed the contortions I was performing right in front of him. I kindly asked him to stretch my muscles apart.

"Uh, Bear?"

"Yeah?" (He continued to look down at the schoolbook he was reading.)

"Do you think you can help me out a little over here?"

"OH MY GOD!"

He stared at me, wide eyed, and tried to pry my shoulders apart. Poor guy. Strong as he was, Bear couldn't even pull my head forward. I didn't realize my muscles were so strong until I had no control over them. Eventually, we called the nurses who rushed in and gasped in horror at my awkward position. They called in the resident who quickly injected Benadryl into the central line to stop the allergic reaction. My muscles slowly relaxed as the medicine counteracted the reaction I was having. My shoulders, legs and arms slowly released and the control of my muscles returned. Bear continued to watch on, astounded.

Unfortunately, no one took care to write down the incident and I awoke at 5am the next morning to another dystonic reaction. My father walked in to find me twisted and staring at the ceiling with my elbows behind my back. He was not too happy with the medical staff for such a gross oversight. Neither was I. My parents and I decided to have a serious talk with the new head of my oncology team from Dana-Farber, Dr. Kernan.

It is interesting to note that this was one of the times my father really took an active role as an advocate while I was sick. During the last days in the hospital we spoke with the oncologists in meeting rooms at Children's Hospital. My father informed them in no uncertain terms that the poor treatment we had received was completely unacceptable for his son. I was glad to have this unexpected outspokenness.

Sometimes I needed someone like my mother to deal with the technical difficulties of dealing with hospital bureaucracy and physicians. In this instance, what I really needed was for my father to portray just how angry I was at this whole situation. I was furious that trained professionals could screw up so badly. I was frustrated with the unexpected tests, the forgotten Trilafon note, the collapsed lung - I was just too tired to speak up. I was silently pleased with my father's impatience and blunt verbal assault on the oncology team.

It alarms me to think of the patients and their families who aren't fortunate enough to have strong advocates like my parents. There are many families who enter the hospital for the first time under the duress of a serious illness. Maybe it's a person who has just had a stroke and has no family to care for them. Perhaps it's a single mother whose child has just been diagnosed with diabetes. Maybe it's a family whose nineteen-year-old son has just come out of cancer remission. Entering the hospital as a sick patient or family member is scary and confusing for anyone. Without an advocate to ensure respect and humanity in any healthcare setting, I fear for the millions of patients who experience horror stories rather than healing experiences.

Unfortunately, our healthcare system seems to have been devoured by the forces of capitalism and commercialism in recent years. With the rise of HMOs and large hospital conglomerations, physicians are often forced to make hard decisions on patient care. Medical residents are often required to work brutal hours that affect the quality of care they are able to give. Patients may have pages upon pages of paperwork to fill out to fight for this procedure or that drug. Blanketing this whole mess is a growing lack of recognition that both doctors and patients are human. Doctors are capable of making mistakes. Yet it is their responsibility, as the healthcare provider and saner counterpart of this human interaction, to treat patients as more than just a chart and diagnosis.

My father voiced these concerns to Dr. Kieran. He voiced them in a gruff voice that illustrated my animosity toward the care I had received. I can forgive a physician for making a mistake, but something in this system has to change. What if my mother hadn't fought for the x-ray that uncovered the collapsed lung? What if the allergic reaction had been fatal? Without a change in the way we train our doctors and monetary incentives in the healthcare system, I pray no one I love need enter a hospital without an advocate.

Add to this dilemma the medical-legal implications of the society we now live in. As physicians are required to squeeze more patients into each workday, they inevitably make more mistakes. Couple this fact with the growing propensity for Americans to seek legal remedies to their problems and we have a situation ripe for disaster. In fact, in many states around the country, doctors are increasingly forced to move or stop doing procedures because they can no longer afford the liability insurance. For example, in Massachusetts, obstetricians often pay over $100,000 a year in liability insurance alone. This decrease in overall care adds to the patient load of those physicians still trying to deliver babies which leads to more mistakes, which leads to more lawsuits. This system will have to change before it completely collapses.

    Within a few days, an overtired resident entered my room and removed the chest tube from between my ribs. A day or two later Dr. Kieran came to my room with discharge orders. My lung had healed sufficiently to leave the hospital. My shackles were released and I was able to finally go home.

Chapter 12

"I know God will not give me anything I can't handle. I just wish that He didn't trust me so much."

- Unknown, commonly attributed to Mother Teresa

Outside the four-paned window my father's pink tree was in various stages of bloom. The uppermost branches were alive with soft flowers that flittered in the breeze. The lower limbs sprouted tiny red buds that waited to come alive. With a few more weeks of sun, the tree would be dressed in complete brilliance. Birds were already making their way back for spring and many found a temporary resting place in this tree. If only for a moment, they needed to rest, to regain strength.

I watched the birds from my bed as they swooped in, sat awhile amongst the crimson buds, and then flew away when their vigor was replenished. Like our feathered friends, I was hoping to find the strength to continue. I longed to fly away back to the freedom I had enjoyed before the cancer came back.

However, the exuberance I felt after leaving the hospital was quickly tempered by the waves of pain I experienced upon arriving in Wareham. I felt like a locomotive had hit me. My chest seared with pain, my bones ached to the marrow and my mouth was full of open lesions. The chemotherapy ravaged my body for the week that I was in the hospital and by the time I was discharged, my blood cell counts had plummeted. Vomiting, migraines, weakness, confusion, and pain that I'd never before experienced made each day an exercise in survival. It was difficult to breathe and I was still adjusting to two rubber hoses dangling from a hole in my chest.

The worst part was the exhaustion. I was simply too weak to do much more than walk to the kitchen and back. I'd struggle to the bathroom only to break out in a sweat at the effort of it all. However, lying in the same position for two or three days began to drive me insane. As I shifted uncomfortably on my uninjured side, the boredom of inactivity allowed me to wallow in self-pity and pain. The chemotherapy left me without the concentration to read and without the ability to walk out of the house. My attitude spiraled into anger and frustration with a side of depression.

My new confines presented another set of obstacles to overcome. The most painful was an injection designed to speed the recovery of my white blood cells. The medicine had the rare-side effect of making my bones ache. I'm not talking slight-discomfort-worked-out-too-hard pain. I'm talking down-to-the-core-of-my-bones-damn-that-hurts pain. My lower back literally felt like it was smashed by a baseball bat. It hurt to stand, to bend - to do anything.

The shot itself was self-injected and it seemed quite a conflict of interest to inflict pain on myself in the midst of such physical and emotional trauma. The visiting nurses taught me how to sterilize my leg and draw the correct amount of liquid from the vial into the syringe. Not only did this stuff destroy my spine but it was also alcohol based and stung like hell under the skin. My mom and I tried to numb the area with an ice cube, which did nothing to dull the pain but it did make my leg cold.

The oddest side effect of the chemotherapy was the loss of feeling in my hands and feet. Actually, it was more like pins and needles than numbness because I certainly could feel it. It doesn't sound bad in comparison to everything else, but just stop and try to imagine sleeping or even relaxing, with pins and needles that won't go away. The constant pricking in my fingertips and toes drove me mad and nothing could stop it. The unrelenting nature of this phenomenon continued to reinforce a sense of helplessness.

The last obstacle was not so distressing physically as it was mentally. I came home from the hospital with two white hoses in my chest. The entrance wound had to be cleaned and re-bandaged every morning and each night. At first, the visiting nurses that came to my home were also in charge of uncovering this lingering reminder of horror. They poked it, inspected it, rubbed it with iodine and finally swathed it in gauze and tape until they came again.

As my strength slowly returned, they showed me how to re-bandage the hole myself. Each morning and night, I needed to wash my hands, put on latex gloves and inspect the entrance of the poisons that did this to me. Each morning and night I was reminded of what I was going through. Each morning and night I realized I was fighting for my life. I knew this was not yet over and the worst was yet to come. I bet you're wondering if it hurt. The answer is "no." After a while it didn't hurt to poke and prod the opening. However, cleaning this hole in my heart never quite felt normal. It didn't hurt, but I felt it and it reminded me that I wasn't the same.

After three agonizing weeks at home, I finally started to improve. I began to stand and walk around without feeling nauseous. I was even able to drive my mother crazy again. Much of the time was wasted lying around watching television and trying to eat a little bit here and there. Not every meal was successful, however, and I mostly stuck to toast and Gatorade. Anything else I ate had a propensity to be a projectile.

At first, Heather still came by to see me and her visits reminded me how loyal she had been during my first rounds of chemotherapy the previous year. I have always been so thankful and indebted to her for all the time she stood by me. However, as teenage relationships tend to go, Heather and I had grown apart while I was at Dartmouth. Our juvenile relationship was unable to overcome the differences we faced as I grew into my college persona and she struggled with high school life. As the weeks past, Heather grew increasingly resentful of being tied to someone who couldn't party with her during her last year in high school. It was hard to see her disappear, but she was only a senior in high school, and I'm not sure what I should have expected. Our relationship stayed cordial and we are still friends to this day.

As the weeks passed, I began to find myself feeling more like a trapped animal. Caged in my house, I began to go stir-crazy. I was too weak to walk past the end of the street before I had to rest and head back. My suppressed immune system made it unwise for me to be around large crowds. My mother was home most of the day, every day; every single day. She seemed ever-present and being, well, motherly. As my strength slowly returned, I began to take out frustrations on the only person who was always around - my mom. Our relationship became even more strained at this point and it continued this way throughout my treatment and recovery. We moved my bedroom back downstairs, now that I had the strength to climb them, and hoped that would help.

I had gone from the autonomy of college dorm life to being imprisoned by my house and the effects of chemotherapy. Having barely transcended adolescence into adulthood, I was thrust back into life as a dependent. My freedom was being withheld through no fault of my own. My mother surely absorbed the brunt of my aggravation as I longed to be on my own again. Cancer handed the stiff sentence of hard time with my cell mate chemo – with no possibility for parole. I was weak, frustrated and scared.

During this time at home, I began deliberating over my options. All of the doctors had given their final opinions. While I recuperated, it was my job to weigh the choices that we had been given. Like anyone in such a grave situation, I'd wished that there could be some magical force guiding my decisions. I hoped that the doctors would know what to do. I expected someone to tell me which pills I needed to take to beat this cancer. That was not the case; it rarely is.

I reviewed the options with my parents. These were the two choices I had to decide between: The team of doctors from the Dana-Farber Cancer Institute said I needed to undergo the transplant as soon as possible to increase my chances for a cure. Dr. Schenkein suggested I wait until they understood my immune system better.

With these conflicting considerations, I needed to make a final decision.

Do I go through with the transplant? They said I might not make it through. Do I wait? But I want to be cured! How long should I put this off? It just doesn't make any sense. Someone tell me what to do! One guy is telling me to do it right away, another person is telling me to wait for a while, and I just don't know what to do!

I was so distraught, so confused, so stressed and depressed. I found myself sobbing in bed every night. I would appear sane during the day when I had other things to occupy my mind. My friends, the mall, and the movies distracted me and allowed me to deny the personal hell waging war in my head each night. The surgical mask I had to wear reminded me that I was still "not normal".

As the lights went off and my head hit the pillow, dark thoughts began to melt their way back into my head. All the fears and anxiety of such a consequential judgment played heavily with my emotions. I kept weighing the options in my mind, and couldn't deny the fact that no option seemed right. As with most important decisions, there were pros and cons for each one.

I can't just "do nothing". I can't just wait. My will to live and stubbornness won't allow me to sit idly by and let fate make my decisions. That's not an option. But Dr. Schenkein thinks the transplant will be too dangerous to undergo immediately. I trust his opinion. I trust him. So, do I wait this thing out and have a few months, maybe a year of chemo free living. Will that give me a better quality of life? If I wait until I'm so riddled with cancer that I have no choice left, the experts in Boston said my chances for a full cure are virtually zero. I have to choose between hope of a full cure or to undergo the transplant right away while I'm still healthy. AGH! What should I do?

I went to bed every night with these feelings and opinions bouncing in my head like billiard balls. I attempted to rationalize each decision and the possible consequences. I'd lie in bed crying, tortured by these thoughts. Even during the day when my mind was focused on other things, a general air of anxiety and frustration gripped me. I was more sarcastic, moody, restless, irritable, and generally rather unstable.

During one particular night, I finally expressed how distressed I truly was. While lying downstairs in my bed, I began to get very negative and depressed. I had been crying for at least an hour or so and just couldn't stop. It had started as one of those cries that begin by feeling good - cathartic even. Then something happened. I simply couldn't stop crying. After a while, my head began pounding, my eyes couldn't produce more tears, my throat hurt, and my heart ached. The tears had emptied me. They drained my strength until the faucet ran dry. I was empty.

It was late at night, around three in the morning. I got out of bed and climbed the cold metal spiral staircase in my bare feet. I walked through the kitchen and down the hallway to my parent's room, hesitating at the door because I wasn't sure what I wanted to say. I wasn't sure if I wanted to show them how far I had sunk.

I eventually went into their room and stood by my mother's side of the bed, still crying dry tears. I didn't want to wake them, just to be near them. Standing there, I wanted to scream. I wanted them to take it all away. My mother heard my whimpers and sniffles and woke up. She awakened my father and it was almost as if they had been waiting for me to finally trust them with this dark side.

I had always been so stoic, so stolid - I acted as though things weren't as hard on me as they actually were. I felt as if it was my responsibility to make others feel as comfortable about the situation as I could. My parents always saw the face of courage and bravery. But they knew I was living a life of uncertainty and fear. Perhaps they went along with my show time act to bolster their own courage, but I know now they were just as scared as I was.

It was a relief to realize they had recognized my scheme all along. I lied down between them in silence for a while. I didn't have to say anything. They put their arms around me and helped me to calm down. I felt like a child who goes to sleep in their parents' bed when they are afraid of the dark, or think they heard a monster. I suppose now that perhaps, in fact, I wasn't as far removed from that child as I would like to think.

My fears were certainly of things more real than hearing noises, or being afraid of the dark - yet still as intangible. No, not the boogie-monsters I feared when I was younger, but much worse. They were morbid fears of death, funerals, tumors, uncertainty and pain. These were the reasons I lay awake each night crying myself to sleep.

After a while lying with my parents, I felt better. Things weren't perfect, but I decided I was calm enough to go sleep in my own bed downstairs again. My mother wanted my father to come sleep on the couch down there, but I refused. I felt well enough to go back by myself.

The situation was much like my life then, and now. My parents (and other family and friends) could always be there as a shoulder to cry on. They could lend an ear to listen, or in this case, a bed to sleep on. They could try to comfort me in times of depression or anxiety, but in some intrinsic sense, they could never follow me to where I was. They could never truly live the experience with me.

This is why cancer patients sometimes feel so alone even when they have such helpful support networks. It is not that I didn't appreciate the sincere attempts to help. It's just that they could never be enough to bring me back from that island of loneliness. My fears could be put into words, but never exorcised from within my head. All of my friends and family tried to help as best they could, but in the end, it was just the cancer and me. No one could follow me down those cold, metal stairs into the darkness.

Chapter 13

"If you find a path with no obstacles, it probably doesn't lead anywhere."

- Frank A. Clark

My new basement bedroom offered the luxury of a minimum of windows. The lack of light afforded a dark, quiet cave in which my hibernating skills flourished. It allowed me to sleep in until early afternoon and wake refreshed after spending most of the night morbidly wondering who would show up at my funeral. No clocks hung on the cement walls and only the red digital alarm clock informed me of the hour when my eyes opened. It was a timeless environment in which to make the most difficult decision of my life. It seemed like only days but weeks had passed since the stay at Children's Hospital.

The doctors would soon want an answer. After talking with all of the doctors, and getting as much information as we possibly could, the time finally came to make a choice. I can't recall a specific day or conversation when I made the final decision. The more I contemplated everything, the closer I came to arriving at an actual conclusion. A brook slowly meanders its way to the sea. Its fate is certain - it will inevitably reach its destination. However, the path is never pre-determined. It may pass over green grasses, between tall trees, smooth small stones, but slowly, surely it reaches the sea.

The struggle and anguish I was going through was in itself part of the solution. The longer I contemplated, conceptualized and cried, the more I realized that there was no way I could live a life while terrified of death. After explaining how I felt, a friend told me the story of an ancient god forced to live with an axe hanging over his head.

That's it! That's exactly how I feel. I am trying to imagine a life surrounded by constant fear and uncertainty. That is no kind of life for me.

Each night in my room I fell asleep to nightmares of death. If I waited until I was too sick to have any options, then the situation would have taken any remaining control out of my hands. The choice would be made by the unsentimental hands of fate.

As it was, I owed myself at least a chance of a full and normal life. Therefore, my only choice was to take the risk and go through with the transplant. Some have called my decision courageous, strong, or even brave, but I felt differently. There was a part of me that needed courage and faith, but there was also a part of me that made the decision because I was scared. I was too scared not to do something and continue to live as a tortured slave - a servant to my tormenting mind with its never ending fears. Every night plunged me into depression and visions of my own death. On some level, I felt I had no choice but to escape any way I could.

My parents learned about my decision first, then my sister, then my friends and anyone else that wanted to know. This was not going to be a secret. I wanted everyone to know that I had made up my mind and I planned to get through this. I was going to survive the transplant and was determined to live. I hadn't read any bargain self-help books, but something told me that a public pronouncement would fuel my will to survive.

My father leapt behind my decision and seemed to understand my rationalization. My mother, on the other hand, was immediately apprehensive and thought I had made my decision too quickly. She was convinced I wasn't fully aware of the consequences. She told my father and me that we were being hasty and insisted that we speak once again with the doctors before making any final decisions. On bad days, she pleaded for me to re-think my choice.

While her intentions were good, her actions made things much more difficult. I had finally settled on some form of conclusion after so many restless nights, but she still felt that my decision was rash. I wonder now if she was just afraid - scared to see that I intended to go through with something that had the very real potential to end her son's life.

In retrospect, I believe she would have been equally afraid regardless of the decision I made. To appease her, my father and I had more conversations with the oncologists. They continued to present us with all of the pertinent facts - rates of success, rates of complications, rates of cure, and rates of death. It was during this time of revisiting with the doctors that I learned what had happened to that mysterious letter from Doctor Armitage in Nebraska.

My mother and I were scheduled to return to New England Medical Center to see Dr. Schenkein. She wanted me to be absolutely certain of my decision so we went back to ask Dr. Schenkein to explain the transplant procedure again. This time, Erik asked to join us. He'd been conspicuously absent during my battle with cancer in high school. He'd been so afraid of losing his best friend that he withdrew somewhat, though he tried his hardest to act normal around me. I believe his request to come to see Dr. Schenkein was his way of trying to make it up to me. The three of us piled into the car and drove to Boston.

While waiting for Dr. Schenkein in the exam room, I tried to express my feelings to my mother. She didn't understand.

"Ma, I just want to do it and get it over with. Look, I'm really pretty healthy now. If I wait until it's too late, I'll have no choice. I want to make this decision and get on with my life."

It was at this point, as my mother's nose began to turn red and her eyes welled up, that she pulled an envelope from her purse. My mother had received it many weeks before. However, she hadn't wanted to show it to me for fear that it might have had too strong a bearing on my final decision. She slowly pulled it from her purse, looked at the address and handed it to me. The postmark read "Nebraska". I knew what it pertained to.

In the letter, the Dr. Armitage and his team from Nebraska stated that, in their opinion, "Kyle's chances of surviving another five to ten years without transplant are quite small, and he most certainly will relapse his Lymphoma again and/or have more severe complications due to infection. With bone marrow transplantation, though the experience is extremely small, I believe his chance of two-year disease-free survival is somewhere between 15 and 25%."

I was absolutely floored. I don't think a single rational thought floated through my billions of synapses for at least thirty seconds. Erik sat motionless but his face displayed concern. He wondered what I'd read and why I hadn't said anything yet. Rather than attempt to explain why I felt like jumping out of the 8th floor window, I simply handed the letter over to him.

As Erik's eyes scanned the page, his face began to turn ghostly white. Here this poor teenager was trying to overcome the fear his best friend was going to die by accompanying him on another meaningless appointment and he gets this. His eyes remained on the floor and as he folded the letter I grabbed it and handed it back to my crying mother. I would need time to process this new information.

The appointment with Dr. Schenkein was very businesslike, as I had no energy to act heroic. I listened to his explanation of the transplant procedure again, but little information reached me as I kept reliving the words in that latter over and over again. After a few questions from my mother, we left. I had less saunter to my teenage walk as we left the hospital and walked to the car. No one spoke on the ride home.

After reading that letter, I wasn't so sure my decision was supremely intelligent. There were many thoughts running through my mind, not the least of which was death. An excerpt from my journal says more than I am able to explain:

April 30, 1996

Have you ever thought about death? Have you ever wondered what happens? I mean, everyone says there's heaven, but is it really a place? We're all going to die sometime right? But I think it's unfair for a nineteen-year-old to have to think about it. I don't know, maybe I'm being a baby, maybe my faith is wavering, it's just hard. Sometimes I wish it would all just leave for a while, so I wouldn't have to think. Do you know, rarely do I go more than a few hours without my mind flipping on me and it starts to go ninety miles an hour… and I just can't stop it. I just can't stop thinking! Can't stop thinking.

Chapter 14

"Man is a romantic at heart and will always put aside dull, plodding reason for the excitement of an enigma. As Doc had pointed out, mystery, not logic, is what gives us hope and keeps us believing in a force greater than our own insignificance."
- Peekay in The Power of One,
by Bryce Courtenay

For the next few mornings, I woke up with swollen eyes and a tear stained pillow. The nightmares rose from my basement bedroom into the waking hours. I sat motionless through breakfast, numb through lunch and stiff through dinner. Part of me wanted to retreat back down those spiral stairs into the darkness, yet the other half was petrified to be alone again.
In the end, I woke from this stupor long enough to realize that I was still in the same situation.

The fact that my survival rate without the transplant was so low only reinforced my decision to risk the transplant. I'd made up my mind, though I was understandably uncertain.

Strangely, there was a calm before the storm. Once the oncologists were sure I intended to go through with the transplant, they intensified their efforts to find a bone marrow donor. Finding a donor was the next, and in many ways, most important step in the process. Without someone to donate marrow, my decision would be a moot point. I'd have a meager prognosis and no amount of high dose chemo could save me.

A month or two after leaving Children's Hospital, I seemed to be back to normal. All I could do was wait for the oncologists to find a donor and go through routine tests. I spent the time frolicking with friends and I even visited Dartmouth a few times during the spring term.

It was a bittersweet experience to be back at school again. I got the chance to see friends that I hadn't seen in months, but I also saw everything I was missing. Whenever I got the chance to visit, everyone was very supportive. The students even held a fashion show in my honor to help raise money for my medical care. Rex and my friend, Nana, had been working on setting up a bone marrow donor drive to see if they could help to find me a match. While I appreciated their concern, the most important thing my friends did was distract me from the painful waiting game I found myself in once again.

Dr. Schenkein slowly worked his way through my family to find a suitable bone marrow donor. He first started with my sister. Statistically speaking, Dana had the greatest chance of being a perfect match.

The current medical technology was able to test for six different antigens (characteristics) of a patient's bone marrow. This is called your HLA type.

White blood cells carry a distinguishing fingerprint on their surface called the HLA system

- the human leukocyte antigen system. The HLA fingerprint is composed of a pair of antigens at several sites on the white blood cell - one each inherited from the mother and the father. As of 1996, twenty four different possible antigens had been identified at the HLA-A site, fifty two at the HLA-B site, and twenty at the HLA-DR site. This medical alphabet soup is a little deep for me, but my point is that with two antigens at each site, more than 600 million combinations of HLA antigens are theoretically possible in the general population. Fortunately, some antigens travel only in sets and certain types tend to occur together, thus reducing the number of possible HLA combinations known to occur in the general population.

These antigens are proteins that play a critical role in protecting the body against invading organisms such as bacteria and viruses. At birth, certain white blood cells called T-cells are programmed by the thymus gland to identify all the antigens that belong in that person's body.

When a foreign antigen is encountered, the T-cells summon various components of the immune system to attack and destroy the invading organism. This system works wonderfully for most of us, most of the time. T-cells examine the antigens on incoming cells and label them as "friend" or "foe". Unfortunately, when bone marrow is transplanted from a donor into a bone marrow transplant (BMT) patient, the patient's T-cells examine the cells in the donated marrow and may launch an immune system attack if they perceive the cells to be invaders.

Alternatively, and more commonly, the T-cells in the donor's bone marrow overpower the patient's T-cells. This condition in known as graft-versus-host disease (GVHD) and is a frequent complication of allogeneic transplants. The "graft" is the donated bone marrow and the "host" is the BMT patient or bone marrow recipient. In GVHD, the donor's bone marrow attacks the patient's organ and tissues, impairing their ability to function and increasing the patient's susceptibility to infection. When transplanted into the patient, the donor's T-cells may look at the HLA markers on the patient's cells, identify the cells as "foe" and unleash an attack on the patient's tissues and organs. The visiting T-cells realize they have somehow been transported to a hostile environment. The visiting T-cells then mount a full-scale attack on the BMT patient's organs.

Luckily, GVHD is usually not life threatening. However, it can be a very uncomfortable side effect of an allogeneic bone marrow transplant.

In severe cases it is fatal. Symptoms may include skin rash, blisters, nausea, vomiting, diarrhea, and jaundice. GVHD can also increase the risk of infection. Because the patient's own immune system is suppressed prior to the transplant it cannot launch a counterattack. Approximately fifty-percent of patients undergoing a transplant with a related HLA-matched donor develop GVHD.

Dr. Schenkein and the rest of my medical team were more concerned with first finding a suitable donor – then they'd deal with GVHD. Ironically, the biracial background I was so proud of would make finding a donor more difficult. You see, the HLA types I've described generally follow racial lines. Unfortunately, minority patients often have a more difficult time finding an appropriate bone marrow donor. A Boston Globe analysis revealed that a decade after a $420 million federal program was launched to address a critical lack of minority bone marrow donors, white leukemia patients' chances of receiving transplants outpaced black patients' odds by more than two to one. They reported that "during the program's existence, a white patient initiating an early-stage search for healthy bone marrow has had about a twenty-two percent chance of finding a donor and having a transplant, the only proven cure for the fatal blood cancer. Black patients have had a ten percent chance during that time."

Many factors may influence this statistic. First, there are simply fewer minorities from which to draw bone marrow. However, there is also historical wariness over government funded medical programs. Many would-be-volunteers site the Tuskegee Experiment in which the U.S. Government let dozens of black men die of syphilis without providing the available cure. Other minority groups may encounter fear of Western medicine or suspicions that medical information will be provided to immigration officials. These statistics became even more salient for me as the doctors explained that my biracial background whittled away the potential pool of marrow donors.

Not only did I simply need a donor, I needed as close to a perfect match as possible. Bone marrow transplants do not have the same level of flexibility as heart, liver or lung transplants. Practically speaking, if a patient had to wait for a person with a perfect heart match to die, they likely wouldn't survive. Secondly, heart tissue cannot fight against its host. A person's body may reject the heart, but this is more easily controlled than transplanted bone marrow bent on destroying the body in which it now resides.

The ideal donor's antigens match all six of the patient's. Transplants have been done with five, four, and on rare and desperate occasions three matching antigens, but fewer matches lead to a greater chance for complications. The antigens are passed on from a person's parents. Since three are passed down from the father, and three from the mother, Dana had the greatest odds of being a suitable match because her marrow could only contain antigens out of a possible twelve – rather than 600 million.

As it turned out, Dana was not a bone marrow match. I imagine she was devastated. She wanted to help her big brother but she couldn't. It wasn't her fault, I mean, she couldn't control her damn HLA type. She simply wasn't a match. As an intelligent twelve year old, she understood the ramifications of not being a match. A few days after the news, I was walking past her partially closed bedroom door when I heard her say to our mother, through her tears, "he's going to die now!"

Yet, Dr. Schenkein and his team still believed that a transplant represented the best chance for a cure. After testing my parents, the doctors made a fortuitous discovery. The three antigens that my mother passed on to me are fairly common in the general population. This meant that at least half of my battle should be easier. My father, however, had antigens that were uncommon. Therefore, the physicians decided to begin the search by testing my father's two brothers and parents.

Cathy, a family friend, is a phlebotomist at the local hospital and offered to draw the blood for the tests at my grandparent's house. She drew blood from my grandparents and uncles and sent the vials to the lab. After further analysis, we discovered that my father's brother, Jonny Roderick, had some of the same antigens as my father, but he was not a close enough match. In a last ditch effort, Dr. Schenkein asked if Jonny's daughter, Jessica, could be tested. Jessica also comes from a biracial background. Like my mom, Auntie Nancy is white, but is unrelated to us. Therefore, the chances that Jessica would be a suitable donor were astronomical. Her mother most likely had an unrelated HLA types.

Jonny and Nancy let Jessica donate a blood sample and we sent the vial back to the laboratory. Given such horrible odds of finding a suitable donor in the registry, Jessica was my last hope. Sometimes fate defies the odds. Sometimes the percentages lie. Amidst a terrible situation, we finally caught a lucky break. When we realized she was a match, I began to feel like things might work out after all. Two months into the waiting game, we discovered that my first cousin, Jessica Roderick, was a perfect match. I had new found hope and was determined to beat this thing once and for all.

The entire family considered this turn of events a miracle - no one more so than my mom. To her, Jessica's wonderfully matching marrow was a sign that serendipity had stepped in to offer her son a fighting chance. I am not sure what it meant to me. Don't get me wrong, I was happy as a clam. I was relieved there was someone to lend me a few ounces of bone marrow. However, something in me always believed that finding blood wasn't going to be the most difficult part. Perhaps I was unconcerned about finding a donor because the search had been so short. Most likely, I was just a naïve son of a bitch. Whatever the case, I was not ecstatic. I should have been weeping with joy, but in this miracle I focused on something besides fate. Now that I had a bone marrow donor, a perfect match no less, there was absolutely nothing to prevent this drama from unfolding. There was no reason to wait any longer. There was no way to avoid whatever might await me at the hospital – for better or worse.

Chapter 15

"I'm not afraid to die. I just don't want to be there when it happens. It is impossible to experience one's death objectively and still carry a tune."
- Woody Allen

By the end of May, my friends began returning from their freshmen years at college. I was selfishly jealous of the stories they told and accounts of adventures they'd had while I was stuck in my basement. Behind my smile I still yearned to be the normal beer guzzling, all night paper writing, girl meeting, mistake making eighteen-year-old they were. Despite the resentment of my situation, I was happy to have my old cronies back in Wareham to keep me company.

I was finally healthy enough to get out of the house and this had a positive effect on my relationship with my mother. I was able to scramble out of her way and she was out of mine. I began doing all the same things most of my friends were doing. I went to the mall, caught the latest movies, hung out, and partied. I basically began acting as if nothing else was going on. Of course, there was something else going on.

I behaved like a young man who didn't carry an enormous boulder in the pit of his stomach. My trips to the mall and movies masked the gravel crunching in my abdomen each night. I certainly felt better since I made the decision to go through with the transplant, but I was still terrified. Ghostly thoughts visited me each night. The weight was still there.

It would be impossible for me to sit here, removed from the situation, and psychoanalyze the many thoughts that flitted though my brain. Emotions swirled through my head like dry leaves on a blustery fall day - swirling and rustling, only settling and stable for a moment before the next gust arrived. Emotions materialized in various, sometimes-contradictory forms. I was angry, grateful, anxious, contemplative, confused, restless, tired, rebellious, stoic, scared, selfish, and at times, depressed. Rocks sat in my stomach, dry leaves twirled in my head.

Throughout the course of the summer, these emotions made themselves apparent as I oscillated from one mood to the next. They permeated my everyday life in a manner that I didn't recognize, but in very real and tangible ways. The most obvious of these was the strained relationship with my mother. She was abused by each mood in turn. If I was angry, she did her best to stay out of my way. If I was rebellious, she laid awake late into the night waiting for me to come home. If I was depressed, she listened to me complain about some problem that was blown out of proportion.

To begin with, the ideas running through the head of a nineteen-year-old boy are rarely coherent for long. Between the hormones, the pressure to become a man and confusion over his place in the world, a teenage boy is barely ever fully sane. However, the issues facing a boy dealing with the possibility of a bone marrow transplant were distinctly different. Each day was spent fraught with tension and anxiety that were foreign to me before I discovered the cancer had relapsed. Part of this disquietude and distress was present when I was first diagnosed with Lymphoma. Yet, the intensity of fear and other emotions was far more profound than the first battle and I felt myself drifting on a sea of confusion.

In an attempt to wield some control during this tumultuous time, I spent my days doing anything that made me feel good. I knew I only controlled my destiny for a short precious time before I entered the hospital. In a few weeks, my life would be in the hands of the chemicals that would mingle and dance with my blood. Daily choices are often taken for granted, but I had been through this before. I knew that the drugs those doctors dripped through the IV would soon oppress the natural ability to control my body and mind. Once the chemotherapy took over I would lose the ability to make my own choices – when to wake up, when to go to the bathroom, when to feel hungry, when to talk to loved ones. There is a loss of control, freedom of movement, ability to socialize and interact with loved one. Therefore, I felt obliged to exert every ounce of personal freedom while it was still possible.

This attitude deeply disturbed my mother and made life difficult for both of us. Let me clarify this a bit. I didn't turn to drugs, sex, or alcohol as a form of escapism. Rather, I simply disregarded anything that got in the way of spending time with friends, partying, or enjoying my last few months of the summer. I ignored, on some superficial level, the deep depression and fears of cancer by immersing myself into a buzzing social calendar. Remaining occupied helped to prevent me from brooding. So, I stayed out late at night, took off early in the morning and didn't come back all day. I was on the phone at all hours of the night, and kept busy to stave off the thoughts that clustered in the back of my mind – waiting to burst out.

In truth, the attempt, while adventurous, was unsuccessful in distracting me. No matter how hard I tried I couldn't forget that I was battling cancer. The harder I played during the day, the more difficult the realizations appeared when my head hit the pillow at night.

Grave thoughts spilled into my mind. *This isn't going away. I have to face it, I'm going to the hospital in just a few weeks. I don't know what's going to happen. What if I die? I wonder who'll be at my funeral. Hell, I need to get to sleep.*

These thoughts continued until the wee hours of the morning.

As hard as their hearts must have wanted to, neither of my parents could understand what was racing through my head. However, it was their role to support me mentally and emotionally. They approached me from two different angles.

My father usually stayed out of my hair and realized I needed to vent in my own way. He made it clear I had his full love and support.

Certainly, at times he had no idea what to say to me but I don't know if I would have asked anything else of him. He showed he cared, let me know he was there if I wanted to talk, and kept things at that. Deep down I imagine he was concerned about my late nights and partying. I'm sure he worried about my heroic ability to ignore the situation, but he gave me the credit and trust to live my own life.

Sometimes I wonder if his distance was as well calculated as I've portrayed, but it's what I wanted at the time. I imagine a father watching his revered son slipping into a treacherous situation. When I waltzed into the house as dew formed on morning grass and he heard my mother launch into me, I wonder what he thought. "I wish Kyle would take better care of himself, but he's old enough now to make his own decisions. I love him so much, I don't know what to say. What should I say to my son who is fighting cancer? I cannot lose my only son."

My mother, in contrast, was constantly discussing my illness. I can see now that this was the main reason I began to resent her so much. She wanted to talk it out – I didn't. She wanted to discuss lab results and courses of treatment. I just wanted to kiss girls. My mother reminded me to change the dressing on the catheter hanging from my chest. I just wanted to pretend it wasn't there. Each day I went through various stages of denial, outrage, pity and acceptance. Well, acceptance didn't arrive every day, but I tried.

My mother viewed my denial and anger as a scared kid acting out in a way that might be detrimental to his health and wellbeing. She correctly placed my anger, but that was more a symptom of my fear. I was terrified and hadn't yet developed constructive ways to communicate my feelings. Instead, my face showed anger and frustration. I didn't know how else to deal with things at the time.

In the tradition of mothers throughout the course of history, Betty Ann reacted by turning into an overprotective mother. Her intentions were of the purest form. She was my mom and I was her baby boy. However, her constant reminders of my health and situation only intensified the frustration I had.

"You have got to get your sleep, Kyle." "Where are you going? You need to take better care of yourself, be home early." "Did you drink last night? Are you turning to that stuff just to escape your problems?" "You feel hot, do you have a fever? Are you getting sick?"

I realized she meant well, but every time she mentioned my condition and situation something inside me turned sour. I yelled, cursed and likely made her cry on some occasions. My words were often caustic and I'd perfected a terrifically icy "shut up and get off my case" face. Beneath my cold exterior I felt awful because, deep down, I knew she was just exceptionally worried and this was the source of her nagging. I just wanted her off my back. I didn't want to think about my illness every day. Couldn't she see this was the reason I was staying out late? I wanted to forget for a while. Our relationship remained strained over the course of the next two months.

To stay out of her sight, I usually dodged out the house soon after I got up. I spent many hours wandering aimlessly at the mall, catching a matinee or rifling through the sale racks. On nights and weekends, my close friends and I hung out at one person's house or another. We might have a few drinks and listen to music or watch TV. No one knew what would happen once I entered the hospital so the hours were passed in a quiet anxiousness that crept into every word, yet everyone smiled as though we'd just won the lottery. My friends also begged for time. In the weeks leading up to my transplant, the phone rang off the hook. They were all nervous and it seemed that as the summer progressed, things began to revolve around me more than they probably should have. I assume it was my friends' way of appeasing me. I delegated where we'd go, what we'd do, who was invited. It felt terrifically indulgent to be treated like a prince for a few weeks – even if possibly undeserved.

While almost all my friends were stunningly empathetic, there remained a couple who weren't exactly sure how to handle things. One of these few was my best friend Erik. Erik had been through a lot when I was ill in high school. He'd watched his best friend lose his hair, grow weak, pale, and grow increasingly angry. He stuck by me during most of that trying time, only to watch me slip back into a horribly treacherous position. This battle was even more dire and he stood a real chance of losing his life-long best friend and cliff-scooter-jumping friend.

When Erik learned how sick I was getting, he had a difficult time dealing with it and began to distance himself from me. Slowly, Erik became less available. He didn't disappear entirely, he just didn't connect in the same way he always had. The phone calls gradually grew shorter and farther between. We found ourselves with less to talk about and the air hung heavy with uneasiness. He never forgot about me and kept up with how I was doing, but somewhere in there he was distancing himself so it wouldn't hurt so much. I know he didn't do this on purpose, he was far too kind and loyal for that. Sometimes friends and loved ones do this when someone they care about has cancer. Subconsciously, it's our way of shielding ourselves from possible devastation. For me, it was devastation.

Our friendship has never been quite the same since. It was hard for me to have such a close friend back away like that. I was pretty resentful for a time, but as the years have passed, I realized that Erik meant no harm and wasn't acting selfishly. He didn't know how to behave - what to say. His best friend was ill, possibly even dying, and there was nothing he felt he could do to help. I saw it in his eyes when we hung out. He was just as scared as I was. He felt helpless and panicked and for the first time in his life, didn't know what to say to his best friend. He was overwhelmed by his own feelings of fear and uncertainty and didn't know what to say to his friend. I see now that Erik was a representation for many friends who withdrew. It was not because they didn't care, but many of them were going through their own inner turmoil as a result of my diagnosis. They didn't know how to treat me so remained silent. Of course, I cannot know the feelings of others, but I imagine I would be capable of the same actions if the situation were reversed.

What Erik didn't realize is that all he had to do was be there. That's all I wanted from my friends – just to be there. They couldn't take the pain away from my limbs nor my heart. They couldn't cure my disease with their tears or by imploring me to "talk about it, get it out." All I wanted was for them to be there as a foundation from which to fight my physical and mental anguish. Friends and family members want to help but they don't know what to say or do. I think what many patients want is just to be treated normally. Too many things were changing in my life. There were already many new dynamics to navigate. What I needed was for loved ones to treat me as they always had. I needed a laugh. I needed to be teased. I needed someone to make fun of my bald head. I needed to be talked to as if cancer wasn't going to kill me and was merely an obstacle that everyone knew I'd overcome. Erik was only a teenager - he didn't know any better.

It was, however, a rough time to have lost such a big source of support. Luckily, new and old friends stepped in which added to an already formidable support system of relatives and people in the community. Several friends took prominent positions in my team of support. It seems that whenever tragedy strikes, there will be those individuals who step up and want to help. The crew: Jill, Cheryl, Sibby and Bear were my heroes for that particular summer - along with Rex and, most importantly, my extended family.

Jill and Cheryl endured many long nights talking with me on the phone to distract my mind from racing so wildly. I would talk to them for hours and hours until I was so exhausted I would fall asleep as soon as I hung up the phone. As a cancer patient, there was little I could do to quell my fears or fight the illness. Dialogue and release were the only forms of catharsis available and the girls indulged me by letting me talk, whine, or even cry.

"I just don't know what to do, I'm so scared."

"It'll be okay, Kyle. You don't have to act so strong all the time," they'd say.

Unbeknownst to me, Jill and Sibby also secretly prepared a thick photo album with picture collages of my friends to take to the hospital. The pictures outlined a summer filled with life. Snapshots of wild parties, hugging friends, funny faces. Each friend had their own page and they detailed the fun times we'd had over the past few months. The nurses would later look at it and make fun of me for having so many female friends. Hey, what could I say?

Bear and Rex were also incredible throughout the whole ordeal. It's harder in our culture for two men to have serious and emotional discussions - but these two were great. I knew I could count on them to know exactly when I wanted to talk and when I wanted to be distracted. Bear in particular knew just how to tease me when I needed a lift. Of course, there were many other friends I would like to thank for their support, but there are too many to mention by name.

The support and generosity I received during that most difficult time renewed my faith in the magnificence of human compassion. It was a solid foundation that would get me through the tough months ahead. During some quiet time cleaning my basement bedroom, I came across a poster-sized picture frame behind the television stand. The frame contained a picture of about seventy five of my closest friends from Dartmouth. On an overcast spring day, Rex, Nana Ashong, and Shauna Brown gathered many beautiful people upon the steps of ceremonial Dartmouth Hall. Rex sent the print to my mother who enlarged it into a poster. She'd planned to give it to me to hang in the hospital room as a reminder of how many people I had pulling for me and where I wished to return.

On the bottom of the poster were words written in my mother's hand. "When your days are long and lonely . . . Remember Green Key . . . Remember Winter Carnival . . . Remember us. We'll be waiting for you . . . For the good times." I was overcome with a tremendous sense of gratitude for all of those people who stood by my side. This poster symbolize the hundreds of people who sent get well cards and the thousands of prayers recited across the country.

The community of Wareham was also very supportive of our entire family. On May 25th, 1996, friends and relatives of my family held an enormous fish fry at the local VFW to raise money for my medical treatment and associated costs. In all, they sold over 700 tickets to the fish fry and local businesses donated prizes for a raffle.

The people in my small community were generous with their financial and emotional support. My family was also invited to the fish fry. Admittedly, we felt uncomfortable about the whole affair. My father refused to go at first. He felt that we were accepting charity, and he didn't like that idea. However, our relatives and friends explained that our family had been giving money and donating time for years, it was okay to receive for once. Our family needed the extra money to get them through this difficult time. My mother had quit her job and my father was already working overtime. To intensify the financial situation, I would be in New England Medical Center for up to eight weeks and my parents hoped to rent an apartment in the city. We lived an hour away from Boston and my parents wanted to remain close in case any complications arose. There were also innumerable medical expenses and co-payments that accumulated rapidly with each trip to and from the hospitals.

The people and support I met on the day of the fish fry were amazingly motivational. It provided an awesome incentive to know that hundreds of people in Wareham were pulling for me. How could I let that many people down? The local newspaper, The Wareham Courier, even ran a cover page story to help garner support. People arrived at the VFW in droves. Old family friends we hadn't seen in years, relatives from far away, even people who didn't know our family but empathized with our situation drove into the dirt parking lot of the VFW to lend a few dollars and words of encouragement.

As if the generosity were not enough, everyone seemed to be having a fantastic time. The group of friends and family that organized the event wore bright red T-shirts that read, "Kyle's Team" on the chest, above their hearts. They warmly greeted all comers with tickets for fish, chips and a plethora of assorted foodstuffs. It was far from the somber ordeal I had imagined. It was a beautifully sunny and warm summer's day. There was food, music and enough damn hugs and cheek pinching to last an entire lifetime. The smell of food overwhelmed the function hall and chirping birds punctuated conversations. My Uncle Johnny, the family DJ, lent the event a joyous air of jazz and disco music. Faces wore broad smiles.

I'd worried about people approaching me with looks of fear, or worse, pity in their eyes. Instead, I found people who cared about my family and me – they simply wanted to help. It felt strange at first to be the object of such unabashed compassion, but after my parents, Dana and I got settled, we had the time of our lives. The party was like a cookout with everyone we'd ever met – a fundraising version of the television show "This is your life" from the 1950s.

One particular event stands out as an eerily serendipitous moment. One of the organizers, Mrs. Donahue, attempted to convince me to buy a raffle ticket. It was a big joke to all those who could overhear since all the money collected was being donated to a fund for my medical expenses. It was the first no-lose proposition I'd ever encountered. I looked over the sheet of prizes and one line popped off the sheet. Win a trip for two aboard the Spirit of Boston. Cruise into the Boston harbor sunset with cocktails and appetizers. The cruise date was a week before I was scheduled to enter New England Medical Center.

Mrs. Donahue continued to tease me.

"C,mon, Kyle. You have to buy a ticket," she said.

"Don't be cheap," she chided.

"Do I have to? I never win these things," I argued smilingly.

"Kyle, you can't lose. Just buy a ticket would ya?"

I accepted her offer and announced to the gathering crowd that I intended to win the dinner cruise. It would be a fun getaway before I was locked up. Perhaps I'd sail away and never come back. Yet, the chances of winning were slim given the dizzying number of people in attendance.

I went back inside and the evening continued with the flair and jubilation of a wedding reception. Old friends, new friends, we ate and danced for hours. After dinner and the festivities, a member of "Kyle's Team" took the microphone from my Uncle Johnny.

"Pahdon me," she stammered in a thick Boston accent.

"Pahdon me, may I please have your attention. We are going to begin raffling off the prizes now. Please get your raffle tickets out."

I salvaged the tickets from the depths of my pocket and crossed my fingers. One by one, the smaller prizes were raffled off – gift certificates, free haircuts and the like. The last prize was the dinner cruise. Now some people say it was all set up, but I watched with my own two eyes as thousands of little red tickets twirled within the large brass cylinder. Small symbols of hopeful squares danced inside this tube and finally the just-recently-revolving drum rocked to a stop. The woman opened the latched door and pulled a solitary ticket out of the big container. I watched it with my own two eyes. As she read off the numbers, I got chills and the hair stood erect on my arms.

"I won!... I WON!" I yelled, not quite sure I was correct. I checked the numbers on my ticket again to be sure.

No one could believe it. When people realized who was yelling above the din in the function hall, they were amazed. The entire room gave me a standing ovation! "Kyle won. Kyle won!" began to circulate quickly through the hall. It was perhaps another sign that destiny might truly have a plan for little old me. If nothing else, I would enjoy my dinner cruise before kicking the can.

Over the course of the next few weeks, I continued to have an incredible summer and enjoyed my newfound awareness of the world, despite the fears running through my mind. However, as the big day approached, emotions began to intensify. My friends didn't know what to say. My family wasn't sure how to act. I didn't know what to expect or think. Fear was held mostly at bay, but at night it was crippling. I read and reread the brochures about bone marrow transplantation, side effects and prognoses. Dr. Schenkein warned me, as Dr. Shimbara had, that these lists couldn't predict what would happen to me, only the possibilities. The only certainty was that I'd soon be locked away in a hospital room, and I'd experience more misery and pain than any pamphlets could explain. If I did survive, my life would be altered in ways I was unable to imagine. I was cognizant of the fact that these moments would change me forever. I'd either be lying stiff in a coffin, or alive and – different.

The night before I left, all of my friends took me out to Karaoke Night at a local dive bar. I forget the name of the restaurant, but it revolved around a maritime theme and a half-buried captain's wheel greeted visitors outside the front door. A cloud of smoke filled the bar and it reeked of cheap beer. The middle-aged men at the bar wore solemn faces that represented many stories – likely sad stories. A cheesy DJ tried valiantly yet unsuccessfully to recruit participants for karaoke.

For our part, we dove into the songbooks and soon began an evening making fools of ourselves on stage and laughed at each other until we cried. Julie, Erica, Jill, Mary Catherine, Jill's mom, Cheryl, Jen, Sibby and all the girls sang their little hearts out. Bear and I diligently dodged the sign-up sheet – having an unusually strong phobia of public singing.

I was, however, the consummate backup dancer. Bear and I added a touch of humor with a parody of old R&B group arm swinging and two-step dance. My friend Jen performed an amazingly passionate, if somewhat off key, "I Will Survive" to round out the night. As the festivities wound down around one in the morning, the lights came on and illuminated heavily stained tables and cigarette scarred chairs. We slowly gathered our belongings and, as we walked out of the bar, I could sense my friends glancing nervously at each other behind my back. They cast worried looks; as though I were walking toward a danger they could not warn me about.

We all exited together in a swarm of nervous laughter and in turn, I said goodnight to all my friends as they climbed into their cars to drive home. Each friend embraced me strongly - a good, hard hug, as if it was my last. Then they began to cry. I did a good job of not crying and reassured all of them I was going to be all right.

My stoicism had been utterly perfected by now. As I hugged one after the other, I felt as though my ship was boarding. I was off to another world where I would be out of touch, out of sight, and no one knew what awaited. I bid farewell to them all in turn, tearful hugs and mascara stained cheek kisses to boot. Neither my face nor words betrayed any of the complex thoughts sifting through my brain. The only clear thought pervading through the fog was this: I may never see these people again. While I cannot be sure, I imagine they were thinking the exact same thing. I continued smiling and making promises I couldn't be sure to keep, "Oh, don't worry, I'll be okay," but inside, it sounded more like this:

"Now boarding, Mr. Roderick. Please fasten your safety belt and put your tray table in the upright position. You will notice no exit signs at either end of the plane. Should we experience turbulence, there will be no mask to drop from the ceiling. Goodbye and best of luck. Thank you for traveling with Cancer Adventures."

Chapter 16

"I can't die. I'm booked."

- George Burns

The day after karaoke, my parents and I set off on an early morning trek to Boston's New England Medical Center. It was July 20th, 1996. Dana went to stay with her friend, Margaret. My parents didn't want her to witness my admission to the hospital. They decided to leave her in Wareham and pick her up when they returned a few days later. After the late night renditions of the hits of the '80s and '90s, I headed to the university teaching hospital with Musak filled elevators and surgical scrubs. My stomach turned and twisted from the trepidation of the events to come.

My parents must have felt similarly as we nervously made small talk during the hour ride to Boston. My mother's weak scolding of my late night shenanigans rang hollow and my father's jokes were worse than usual. When we arrived in the city we stopped first at my parent's newly rented apartment to drop off some clothes. They would spend their nights in this small room while I was in the hospital. From the apartment, we quickly made our way to the hospital. Bags of poison awaited me this early morning. Fancy expensive chemicals with important sounding names lay sleeping in their plastic clothes until I arrived.

Dr. Schenkein met us as we arrived at the hospital. This place was not the other-worldly environment at Children's hospital. For one, there was carpeting. You may not think it, but what a difference a little area rug can make. Secondly, Dr. Schenkein treated us like human beings when we sat down with him. Finally - the walls – they weren't all white! The only thing that bound this place to the experience of other hospitals was the smell. There is always that sterilized institution smell.

It was so early that the regular oncology clinic was still closed so we sat alone with Dr. Schenkein. An odd sense of importance hung in the air around us. Dr. Schenkein re-explained the protocol for the upcoming week. I'd receive eight days of copious amounts of chemotherapy. Schenkein called it the "conditioning regimen". One might assume that a conditioning regimen would get someone in shape. In marathon training, this might connote getting in shape. What it meant to me was nine days of poisoning, intended to kill cancerous cells. During this process, it would also destroy the bone marrow I'd been producing my entire life.

If this went smoothly, the chemicals would kill every cancer cell and destroy all traces of my bone marrow. Jessica's marrow would then be harvested, "cleaned" on the tenth day and subsequently injected into my bloodstream. From there, the marrow cells would find their way into the large cavities of my bones and (hopefully) replace the cells killed by the toxic fluids. Dr. Schenkein had already given me books on what the procedures and chemo would make me feel like, so we only briefly went over them.

After we signed some papers, Dr. Schenkein walked us out of the clinic, down the hall, and through the closed doors of the Bone Marrow Transplantation wing. A tall nurse approached us and introduced herself. "Hi, Kyle, Mr. and Mrs. Roderick, I'm Amy. I am going to be your head nurse." I felt a sense of shock and disbelief of the situation as I investigated the sights and sounds of the bone marrow wing. Many charts and schedules hung upon the wall and men and women buzzed through the hallways.

My attention finally drifted back to Amy as she ushered my parents and me into the quarters where I'd spend the next month. My first impression of the room was that it seemed rather comfortable, all things considered. "It's no Ritz, but it'll do," I thought. New England Medical Center had just recently finished building this portion of the hospital and everything glimmered with newness. The room was moderately sized - maybe fifteen feet by twenty. Conveniently, it was a little larger than my last dorm room. It was bigger AND had no roommates!

Opposite the door was a large window that stretched from wall to wall and almost to the floor. Looking out the window, rooms of another wing of the hospital peered back. Beside the wing wove the Boston expressway with its notoriously bad traffic. Above the hospital stood some of the taller buildings in Boston with the harbor filling in the rest of the background. If not for my current location, I'd have enjoyed the view.

Along the wall to my right were a sink and mirror and a lightly stained pine closet. A similar closet and some drawers stood to the right of the sink. Up in the left-hand corner, above the closet and near window, was a seventeen inch television and VCR suspended from the ceiling. To my left was an electric bed jutting out from the middle of the gray and maroon wall. The bed sported standard bleached white sheets and faux-wood paneling with a nifty set of handrails. Between the bed and window rested a small bed table with a beige colored telephone and three drawers.

The wall surrounding the bed resembled the control panel of a spaceship. The variety of blood pressure cuffs, containers, instruments, injectors, labels, masks, metal hooks, pumps, plugs, outlets, rubber hoses and switches upon the wall produced a dizzying medical spectacle. I'll admit I was bewildered by the possible necessity of the myriad of instruments in that room. *Will they need all that crap for ME?* The machinations stared coldly from the wall without reply.

As I stepped further into the room I noticed that there was also a decently sized bathroom behind me to the left. It was clean as a whistle with a tile floor and walls, toilet, sink, mirror and a shower with a seat. *A shower with a seat? What the hell would I need a seat in the shower for?* I'd soon find out.

"Mr. Roderick, we have taxied and are preparing to take-off. The captain has turned on the 'fasten seatbelt' sign and requests you stay in your seat for approximately one month. You'll notice a variety of controls above your seat. We don't know what they do yet, but best of luck. Buckle up!"

I'd arrived with a small suitcase full of specially laundered clothes. *"There is no way I am going to wear those ugly johnnies every day!"* I also brought the aforementioned picture of Dartmouth classmates, a Walkman, magazines, a laptop computer and a pad of paper to write letters. That's it. I couldn't think of anything else to bring to occupy me so I'd have to find a way to make do. Amy gave my parents and me a moment to store my belongings and take a deep breath. However, she warned us that we only had but a few minutes before they'd be ready to start chemotherapy again.

So here we stood on day number one. It was difficult to launch immediately into the medical procedures, but in a masochistic way, I was glad to finally start the process I'd dreaded for so many weeks. Anticipation often breeds fear more efficiently than actual risk. In this case, I'm not sure whether anticipation could truly overestimate the danger but I suppose that's beside the point. I was there and we were going to get into this thing.

The next stage of my journey started a few minutes later. It was a Saturday – Sabbath for some, menacing for me. The protocol was a complicated schedule of name brand poisons produced in a laboratory, designed to save my life. They had names that conjured images of military dictators from far-off, warn-torn countries - or of secret weapons built to annihilate those countries.

On Saturday the physicians first gave me Busulfan tablets. Busulfan is an oral chemotherapy that can take the place of radiation. Thursday (day six) they would pump in VP 16, which is also called Etoposide. It was on to Cytoxan Friday and Saturday. We took a spin on the gamma globulin ride, Sunday, to help ward off infection. Then the actual transplant on Monday, July 29, 1996.

Cytoxan? Etoposide? This is supposed to be saving my life? They sound horrific. Don't the pharmaceutical companies ever run these names through a focus group?

The first few days passed with ease. Nausea and other mild side effects were easily controlled with drugs like Zofran, an anti-vomiting medication. I'd flirted with the nurses sufficiently to secure a place as one of the ward favorites. At least, that's what they told me. When not feeling sick to my stomach I'd managed to write a few letters and watched an obscene amount of television.

In this first stage, before my white blood cell count dropped, I was allowed to entertain a few visitors and leave my room. My buddy, Cheryl Gillpatrick, came up to visit during this phase and I was happy to interact with someone other than my parents. I imagine they also welcomed the break from sitting in the room with me.

"Ma, I'm going for a walk with Cheryl, alright? We'll be back in no time."

When the words came out of my mouth, I had truly intended to stay in the hospital. However, as we approached the windows toward the elevator, I saw what a beautifully sunny August day had materialized in Boston. On the city streets below, people waltzed the avenues in shorts and T-shirts. I watched jealously as lovers strolled arm in arm down the street. I'd already been locked in my room for two or three straight days and was not yet used to the isolation. I just needed to get out.

I had nothing to lose. I mean, I was going to be locked in my room for at least four weeks – maybe longer. Who knows, I might not even be around once these chemicals got a hold of my body. I wasn't staying in that goddamn hospital when it was so gorgeous outside.

Sporting a plastic hospital bracelet and self-serving rationalization, I strode through the revolving glass doors to freedom. Cheryl paused inside. A look of incredulity came across her face from behind the glass. She raised her hands, palms up, as if to say, "What the hell do you think you're doing?" With a toothy smile and a sideways nod, I beckoned her outside. She pushed her way through the revolving doors and said, well, "What the hell do you think you're doing?"

I answered her simply by walking away from the hospital. I didn't have a plan, but thought walking in the sunshine was a most marvelous thing to do on such a day. Within minutes we found ourselves meandering through Boston's Chinatown. We perused oddities in the windows of family owned shops. We chitchatted about friends in Wareham and I asked Cheryl to pass along well wishes.

    We continued walking out of Chinatown and into the Boston Common. After strolling through the grasses of the Commons we crossed Charles Street into the Public Gardens. The Gardens are a manicured floral exposition with a swan pond rested serenely in the center. As we entered the main gates, I was moved as I studied the vibrant flowers, watched parents walking their children, smelled fragrances of flora, heard birds chirping merrily and blissfully ignored cars honking in the background. Ah, Boston drivers never disappoint. The smells, sights, and sounds smacked my senses like Muhammad Ali in Manila. Cute blonde-haired high-schoolers sold lemonade from street corners. Clowns smelling of cheap whiskey fashioned poodles out of balloons. Life could not be sweeter.

    This experience has become etched in my mind as one of the most intense events of my life thus far. Outside in the fresh (well mostly fresh) air and sunshine, I realized there was a very real possibility I would never see beyond the hospital walls again. I was overwhelmingly anxious, nervous and terrified with what could happen. However, what I realized as Cheryl and I waltzed amongst the flowers was that I had just been handed an important life lesson. In deciding to walk out the revolving hospital doors that day, I learned something important about living each day to the fullest and seizing opportunities when they arise. If I had not ventured outside and something had happened to me (like death), it would have been an absolute tragedy. I learned no one can predict the future. All we have is the present. My decision to walk out that day, to live, will affect the rest of my life.

Cheryl and I continued to walk around the park, and even contemplated taking a ride on the swan boats in the pond, but decided that we might be pressing our luck. Instead, we each got a Slush Puppie from a vendor on the sidewalk and took our time meandering back to the hospital.

"Where have you been? You've been gone for almost two hours!" my mother screamed as we entered my hospital room.

"Aw, just walking around. Looking at stuff", I said as I sent a sidelong wink to Cheryl. My mother never figured out that we'd left the hospital until she read the first draft of this book.

The next few days went smoothly, but I grew increasingly ill from the immense doses of chemotherapy. I spent much of the time in the hospital bed watching television, writing letters, reading magazines and talking with the nurses. These first two weeks I got to know my primary nurses - Amy, Jen and Karen. They were incredibly sweet and made my stay as comfortable as they could. Amy was the smart head nurse, Karen was the prettiest, but Jen was the funniest and probably my favorite. All three were younger and teased me incessantly about all the pictures of young women I had in my photo album.

At first, it was impossible to feel comfortable as I endured the embarrassing procedures the nurses had to perform. We have many societal norms that prescribe boundaries of privacy and discretion. In a hospital, the same rules do not apply. Patients are forced to allow their caregivers to perform ignoble medical procedures that we'd normally deem extremely awkward if not obscene. However, I had to learn to disregard my pride and admit that I couldn't do it all alone.

On the bad days, I found myself too weak to crawl five feet into the bathroom or dress myself. Jen, Amy and Karen were there to assist me or allow me to lean on them mentally and physically. If I'd been healthy, the treatment certainly would have seemed intrusive and greatly unwelcome. As it was, I reluctantly agreed to allow the nurses I adored to help me into the bathroom. The bond between patient and nurse grew rapidly as I struggled through such extraordinary circumstances. Three friendly faces greeted me and lent strength each day I woke up in the misery of the transplant room. Almost as survivors of a tragedy come to regard each other in very intimate terms, I perceived these women as partners in my struggle.

When I was particularly stressed or in pain, I pressed the unassuming plastic call button that was strapped to my nifty handrails. That red button was often times a lifeline as I writhed in pain. I'd call for Jen or Karen because I knew they'd find a way to force a smile. Jen told the craziest stories and funniest jokes. Sometimes she'd simply make fun of me so I'd laugh. Humor most certainly helped as much as the chemicals flowing through my veins. I loved it. My favorite story was the one that explained the large bandage on Jen's arm. As she recounted how her mountain bike had slipped from beneath her and she was launched into the air, I found myself laughing at her outrageous descriptions of flying body parts and earth.

Karen was both attractive and gregarious. A small amount of attention lifted my spirits and renewed my determination. Within no time I'd developed a schoolboy crush on both of them. Their compassion treated both my body and mind. Their warmness soothed my mind in a way in which no salve or pill could compete.

However, despite the beautiful people who cared for me, the chemicals weren't designed to perform gently if they were to work. Thursday, day six, the doctors carried in Cytoxan. With it, they sentenced me to the most humiliating experience thus far. Cytoxan is a potent chemotherapy agent. If it was not flushed quickly from my bladder it could severely damage the tissue and cause irreparable scarring.

My favorite nurses prepped me for treatment by inserting a catheter to help drain my bladder. I'm sure I needn't explain to you how they insert a catheter into a man's bladder – it was painful. These same women I joked with each morning, talked with each evening, violated me in a most personal way. It's a job they've each done dozens of times before, but it was my first. It was not so much the embarrassment of having grown women manipulating my genitals as it was a loss of control over my own body. I didn't move much during the twenty-four hours I was attached to the catheter. The pain radiated throughout my being as I lay helplessly – hoping desperately that I'd made the right decision.

When I'd first entered the hospital, Amy explained to my parents that it would take around a week for the major side effects to take hold. As day seven approached, I became increasingly fatigued and irritable. My strength slowly but steadily faded. I required more attention and assistance. Getting up to brush my teeth was becoming difficult and sometimes I needed Jen or Amy to help me stand so that I wouldn't pass out – minty foam trailing from my mouth. Instead of jokes to bolster my spirit, I needed someone to hold my arm lest I fall down. My sense of autonomy and privacy was eroding like a sandcastle at the edge of high tide. I tried desperately to maintain a façade of strength and independence.

Gradually, the frequency and duration of queasiness and pain increased but the worst side effect was the loss of concentration. On the eighth day, as my concentration continued flagging, I reached my first major obstacle. My biggest fear other than death was a loss of mental control. It is only natural to fear intellectual deterioration. Who we are is simply an amalgam of what we think. As the days dragged on and my ability to concentrate during conversations deteriorated, I was completely unnerved. My sense of self was being threatened as I struggled to maintain a coherent thought.

My ability to read and write deteriorated first and I grew frustrated as I reread sentences over and over without meaning. Before I'd finish a paragraph I'd forgotten what I was reading. Thoughts continued to grow more fragmented and disjointed. I spoke to friends on the phone, only to forget my point mid-sentence. I even had difficulty attending to the television. Practically speaking, I witnessed myself get stupid in real time. Unfortunately, it would get much, much worse before it got better.

Why can't I concentrate? I can't even read this stupid article. I'm a smart kid, I can't believe I feel so dumb! I can't even talk to my parents without sounding like an idiot. I feel so confused. This is ridiculous! These chemicals are completely screwing with me. Will this be permanent? Ugh, I feel sick.

On the ninth day, nothing happened. The chemotherapy was over and now the waiting game resumed. The absence of chemo afforded me a nauseous free day and a welcomed reprieve from the hordes of physicians and the entourage that stormed my room. I felt pretty well - all things considered. Tomorrow was a big day for me.

After a restful night's sleep, Monday, July 29th finally arrived. It was transplant day. My cousin, Jessica, arrived at New England Medical in the early morning. After signing the required forms, the doctors anesthetized her and began pillaging her hips for bone marrow.

With the same large needles they used on me a few months prior, they extracted several ounces of her bone marrow from the hind part of her pelvis. They harvested between one and two quarts. While this may sound like a lot, it represents approximately two percent of her total bone marrow volume. That was all that I was going to get – two percent. Jessica's body would replace that amount in a little under four weeks. The doctors then "cleaned" her marrow by subjecting it to radiation. My weakened immune system would leave me tremendously vulnerable to the bacteria and viruses in Jessica's blood that she was able to fight naturally. The radiation killed those organisms to make the marrow safe to inject into my bloodstream.

On this, the tenth day, a new life was carried to me in an unassuming plastic bag. The doctors walked upstairs at 2pm. Interestingly, introducing the marrow to my body was the most benign procedure I'd seen in weeks. They simply hung this small red bag on a pole and dripped it through IV tubing into my arm. It looked like Ragu spaghetti sauce to be honest. From my bloodstream, the cells began to find their way to the largest cavities in my bones. It's amazing what medical technology can do these days, but

I'm more impressed with Mother Nature's instruction to these small cells that know just where to go. No asking for directions here, thank you very much.

Once settled in the bones, these cells would begin to reproduce and create new white blood cells, red blood cells and platelets. This process is known as "engraftment." Engraftment usually occurs within two to four weeks after transplantation, and is monitored by checking the patient's blood counts on a frequent basis. Complete recovery of immune function takes much longer - up to several months for autologous transplant recipients and one to two years for patients receiving allogeneic transplants.

While receiving the transplant was a small miracle in its own right, the most treacherous days laid ahead. The physicians had just introduced an essentially foreign substance into my body. They remained cautiously observant over the next few hours as the last of the Ragu entered my veins. They were concerned that my body might reject Jessica's marrow. Luckily, things went smoothly and there were no further complications this day. The marrow drip-dropped from the bag, through the pulsing tubes and into my veins. The undulating rhythm of an electronic IV line still reminds me of a heartbeat.

Chapter 17

"We need to be reminded that there is nothing morbid about honestly confronting the thought of life's end and preparing for it so that we may go gracefully and peacefully. The fact is, we cannot truly face life until we have learned to face the fact that it will be taken away from us."
- Billy Graham

When Jessica awoke, nurses wheeled her upstairs to my room. She looked even worse than I did because the anesthesia made her nauseous. My aunt Nancy accompanied her and I thanked them both for agreeing to donate Jessica's marrow. I'm sure Jessica and her family never thought twice about it, but I was grateful for this precious gift nonetheless. Jessica only stayed a short while in my room because she still felt sick. She went home later that afternoon. My mother sent her home with a bouquet of flowers, which seemed like small consolation.

Receiving Jessica's marrow marked the end of any further chemotherapy treatment. The side effects of the previous 8 days still hadn't reached their full strength but at least the doctors were done pumping those poisons into me. Now it was back to the waiting game once again. Jessica's marrow had to grow strong enough to lend me an immune system that was capable of breathing everyday air. I stood a good chance of catching a life-threatening infection that could ravage my body that stood defenseless again these tiny bacterial and viral invaders. To survive, Jessica's marrow had to reproduce in my body quickly enough to protect me from such an infection – the number one killer in marrow transplantation.

The other big risk factor is graft-versus-host disease (GVHD). If Jessica's bone marrow decided that I wasn't a place it wanted to reside, the transplant would be unsuccessful and I would likely die. If Jessica's bone marrow engrafted before I contracted a serious infection and if I didn't get a fatal case of GVHD, I could be released from the hospital. The nurses visited my room every morning with a needle to check my blood levels.

To prevent serious GVHD, the physicians immediately began infusing me with Cyclosporine. Cyclosporine is one of the most effective anti-rejection drugs of our time. It has certainly helped increase the acceptance rate in many types of transplantation. Dr. Schenkein informed me that I would be on IV Cyclosporine for fifty days. I would need fifty days of the oral version if I made it home.

After the transplant, things grew more interesting by the day. I began getting weaker and losing weight rapidly. The chemotherapy effects were beginning to take their toll. My appetite disappeared within a day or two. By day ten I felt no desire to eat. Arguably, this had as much to do with the quality of the cuisine as my condition, but either way I couldn't choke any of it down.

Every day that went by took a pound or two with it.

At first, I was managing a positive outlook relatively well despite the chemicals ravaging my body from the inside. Still, there were some small problems immediately following the transplant procedure. Something I was taking caused a rash that itched day and night. Dr. Schenkein prescribed intravenous Benadryl to help control the allergic reaction. Unfortunately, the Benadryl made me amazingly sleepy and I felt like I was in a trance all day. I felt guilty as my parents came to visit and I could barely keep my eyes open. Some hours were better than others. I continued to grow weaker and continued to sleep the day away.

On Tuesday (day 12 post transplant), my sister Dana was allowed to visit. We played some silly board game and then I found myself dancing along to the Temptations' song "Get Ready." I was back to singing Motown. The nurses thought it was hysterical and I think Dana enjoyed it too. She was only twelve and I was sure I could fool her. "He's not doing too badly," she must have thought. It was rouse to prove to her that I wasn't very ill. It was a splendid act, but perhaps she wasn't as naïve as I imagined.

Wednesday through Saturday (days thirteen to sixteen) went by without major complications, but my blood counts continued to drop and I grew more fatigued as each day passed. Sunday, I took a turn for the worse, and needed a blood transfusion. My platelet count had dropped dramatically during Saturday night and I needed two whole bags to replace them. The full effects of the chemotherapy were now well underway. Hopefully the chemo was killing all the cancerous cells, but it was decimating my healthy body in the process.

At this point, everyone who entered my room was required to utilize the sanitation station outside my door. An immaculate porcelain sink is surrounded by instructions on how to wash properly, and many boxes of paper masks, gowns, gloves and booties. My own mother stood at that sink and scrubbed her hands with antibacterial soap for a full minute. She'd slipped the plastic hair cover over her head and secured the paper mask that covered her nose and mouth. Next were latex gloves. One sneeze by my mother could kill me – how fragile.

The immune system that nature had given me was gone. If all had gone well, not a single cell that had defended me for twenty years would have survived. Jessica's two percent was the only protection I had. This was my decision – live or die.

On Sunday, I spiked a fever of 103 degrees, my joints and muscles ached, and I told my parents I felt as if I had been beaten up. My head pounded and each sound felt like a jackhammer to my ears. I developed an itchy rash all over my body and the doctors weren't sure where it came from. It could be an allergic reaction to a medication, GVHD, the cytomegalovirus (CMV), or merely irritation from detergent on the sheets.

IV Benadryl helped to stop the itching, but added to the sleepiness.

Dr. Schenkein and his colleagues monitored me closely for CMV. Cytomegalovirus is a virus that causes mild infections in healthy individuals but can be dangerous to immune-suppressed patients. CMV is a member of a group of viruses in the herpes family. It strikes mainly in the lungs and can cause CMV pneumonia, though it can present as colitis or hepatitis as well. Sources vary, but anywhere from fifty to eighty percent of the general population are infected by CMV during their lifetime and almost all of these people are unaware of having the disease. A blood test before a bone marrow transplant can determine whether CMV is present in the patient's body. If not, the patient is "CMV-negative" and care is taken to prevent exposure to CMV. If the patient has been exposed in the past then they are CMV positive and CMV can recur when they are immunosuppressed. CMV occurs in approximately twenty percent of bone marrow transplant recipients and risk of infection is greatest between five and thirteen weeks after transplantation. Anti-viral medications such as immunoglobulins and antibiotics are available to help prevent and treat this virus.

Other common side effects of the conditioning regimen are mouth sores. Shortly after the chemo ended, my mouth and throat began sprouting painful lesions. Even if I had an appetite, it would hurt too much to eat. Mucositis is a common side effect of chemotherapy and radiation.

Inflammation and infection result in mouth sores and a sore throat. Mucositis is so frequent and severe that 80% of patients receive intravenous nutrition and pain medication for the sores. Small white sores soon turned to large white abscesses that coated my cheeks, gums and throat. Amy, Jen and Karen brought me Ativan to ease the pain and calm me down. It seemed that Ativan was a cure-all for the transplant unit and seemed to be given no matter what the complaint.

I was also losing weight because my appetite had vanished. Dr. Schenkein decided that it was time to start feeding me intravenously. My body would need the nutrition to rebuild itself. Every morning, the nurses came in and hung a plastic bag of yellow jelly. This goo was called Total Parenteral Nutrition (TPN) and it provided me with the calories and nutrients I needed to survive. As they hung the bag, I invariably came up with some joke about what was for breakfast. One day it was "yellow steak," the next it was "yellow chicken noodle soup." I may have felt like crap, but I refused to lose my sense of humor.

There was now an IV pole attached to my chest wherever I went. The TPN would flow continuously until I was able to eat solid foods again – which was weeks away. Whenever I went to the bathroom, I had this stupid pole with me. Whenever I rolled over, I was careful not to roll onto the tubes that connected the pole to the hole in my chest. This damn thing would haunt me constantly for the next month and would be around for many more months to come. I swear when I buy my first house, I'm using it as a coat rack. As it turns out, a number of years later, that sucker was in the guest room. Morbid but useful since there was no closet in there.

On Monday morning, I slowly made my way into the bathroom to brush my teeth. I swung one leg out of bed, meekly followed by the other. I clutched at the ever-present IV pole and began a painstaking five-foot journey. I entered the bathroom, turned on the light and looked in the mirror. To my dismay, a bald, pale, scrawny guy stared back at me with blood-red eyes. A lack of platelets allowed broken blood vessels to flood the whites of my eyes until they were completely filled. The sight was horrific and quite frankly scared the hell out of me. My eyes were sunken and red, my face gaunt, and my eyebrows and eyelashes were the only hairs left on my body. I was in rough shape.

By Monday afternoon, my fever had risen and the attending physicians put me on an intravenous morphine pump to control the pain. Dr. Schenkein had left for the week on vacation, but the attending physicians decided that the morphine was necessary. The pump reset every ten minutes so that I could self-regulate the pain medication. While the narcotic effects alleviated the pain, I was beginning to drift away from my parents and friends who called on the phone. My days were spent in an ebb and flow of clear-headedness. A hazy fog descended on me for much of the day, but I didn't care. I just wanted the pain to stop.

Soon, my IV pole had a friend. A shiny metal acquaintance was added to help him mock me. The bags of TPN, platelets, saline, steroids, Cyclosporine and many others overwhelmed the first pole. The nurses needed more hooks to hang their plastic bags on. The shiny friend was ushered in one morning and I swear I heard them snicker. They stood there silently all day and night – sentinels.

I also finally learned what that seat in the shower was for. Remember I thought it was odd when I first arrived? Well, after expending all my energy to cross the five feet to the bathroom, I needed a place to sit. I sat on the toilet as I brushed my teeth, taking a breather every minute or so. After standing up to rinse my mouth, I turned on the shower. I dare say passing out in the shower could be detrimental to one's health and therein lays the magic of the "shower-seat". I breathed heavily as I stripped off my clothes and plopped myself onto the vinyl cushion with the weight of the world on my shoulders. Okay, okay, so it was only a hundred pounds and change, but it felt immense to my weak legs. I didn't have the strength to wash myself just yet and so sat for many minutes until I recovered my breath. This was the hardest damn thing I had ever done.

"Mr. Roderick, Mr. Roderick, we would just like to inform you that we are experiencing some turbulence at this point. Please make sure your seat belt is fastened and hold on."

Tuesday remained the same. The headache and rash intensified and the sustained temperature caused me to sweat profusely. I also began retaining water and soon had gained twenty pounds of fluid. The physicians prescribed Lasix, a diuretic. Unfortunately, imagine yourself lying in terrible pain, with a splitting headache and not enough red blood cells to get to the bathroom without considerable effort. Now imagine that someone has hung both a bag of saline to hydrate you, and IV pushes of Lasix to make you pee. I quickly lost my embarrassment over urinating in the bed pans that Jen and the nurses brought me. It took too much to get to the bathroom so often and I didn't have the energy to care anymore.

On Wednesday my fever rose to 105 degrees and I began to have rigors. Rigors happen when the muscles in the body begin to spasm and shake uncontrollably. The physicians gave me intravenous Demerol to relax the muscles and help manage the pain. The nurses also placed a cooling blanket on me to help keep the temperature down. I didn't sleep a wink Wednesday night regardless of the Morphine and Demerol, and called my parents at 5am to tell them I was in excruciating pain.

"Hello?"

"Dad? I'm not doing so well."

"What's wrong? Are you okay?"

"No, no I'm not okay. I haven't slept all night and everything hurts. I've been lying in bed listening to the clock tick all night and my whole body freaking hurts!"

"Okay, okay, calm down. We'll be there in a couple of hours. Can you hold on until then?"

"Yeah, I guess so, but I don't know how much longer I can take this, Dad . . ."

I do have one pleasant memory from this time. With such a high fever, the nurses and my mother often brought in paper cups filled with ice chips. Through the fog of pain, I remember vividly the feeling of ice chips being placed tenderly into my mouth. They soothed the sores and were the only point of coolness I could feel. Each paper cup was like a small present brought with love from a caring woman. In the midst of the carnage and pain enveloping my body these paper cups seemed like small miracles.

At this time, the team of doctors decided it would be okay to up the dosages of the painkillers and muscle relaxants. Clouds of semi-consciousness rolled in and rained down sleep and hallucinations. Some moments I was lucid, others I seemed drunk. Karen later told me that she came into my room one morning to hear me mumbling.

"What's going on, Kyle?" she asked.

"Karen! So nice to see you. I'm going out to get some coffee, would you like some?"

"You're going out to get some coffee, eh?" she replied with her beautiful smile.

"I sure am. Would you like any?"

"Why yes, cream and sugar please."

"Okay, great," I said, and proceeded to roll over and fall asleep.

On Sunday, day twenty four, I had an acute pulmonary hemorrhage and I might have drowned in my own blood. Luckily, Dr. Schenkein had returned just in time, and gave me a large dose of steroids to control the bleeding. The steroids were definitely one of the worst parts of my time at the hospital. I literally didn't sleep for three whole days. This is when the war began.

The steroids made me extremely wired, agitated, restless, and all of my nerves felt as though they were on fire. I could not sit still. My mind raced so fast that it scared me every minute of the day. As I mentioned, my biggest fear was a loss of control. I could not form thoughts. I could not speak very coherently. When thoughts happened to flash across my mind, they were almost incomprehensible. They didn't make sense and my mind was racing so fast. It was a freakish slide show of insanity stuck on fast forward. It was all I could do to lie in bed and not go crazy. I wanted so desperately for the pain and confusion to go away. I would lay in my hospital bed at night unable to sleep and just sob.

It was almost as if I were crying simply to focus my attention on something. It became like a mantra. My sobs were so deep and heavy-hearted that I was unable to attend to the frenzy in my mind. Hours upon hours were spent each night simply weeping until I was physically exhausted. I tried to control it during the day when people could see or hear me, but at night, crying soothed me.

On one particular day, the madness became too much for me to handle, and with both of my parents in my room, I absolutely lost my mind. I started yelling for the nurse. I told her that I wanted drugs, anything and everything they could give me. I wanted something to make this feeling stop. My parents called for Jen. She arrived quickly at my bedside and tried to talk to me.

"Just make it go away! Make it stop! Knock me out! I want drugs! I don't care, just please make it stop! Make the thoughts go away, Jen. Please help me . . ."

Jen sat down quietly and talked to me soothingly for a while. She asked me if I was in pain or if there was anything else wrong. I informed her that yes, of course I was in pain, but it was my mind that was driving me insane. She helped me to relax a bit and suggested that I take a brief walk with my parents down the hallway. I thought that perhaps getting out of the room might help and sheepishly agreed.

I donned a protective mask and tied my Johnnie. My parents and I slowly walked to the door and out into the hallway. It must have taken me twenty minutes teetering along with the IV pole to walk down the forty foot hallway. We entered the family waiting area and discovered that it was empty. I sat and then lied down on a sofa after my grueling walk down the hall. After about an hour, I relaxed a little more and was even able to laugh.

After I had been released from Children's Hospital following the high dose chemotherapy in April, I had told my parents that I had felt like I had gotten hit with a train.

"Well," I said as I looked at my father.

"Do you know that two mile long train we see on our family trip to the Berkshires every year?

Well, THAT'S the train that I just got hit by, the one a few months ago was just one of those little toy electric trains!"

I let out a brief half-hearted laugh. I realized that this was the real thing, and I was scared - very scared.

Each day continued to bring a series of highs and lows. I would feel on top of the world one minute, wondering why I was even in the hospital. Ten minutes later, my head would begin to spin and I'd feel faint from the lack of erythrocytes feeding my body with oxygen. Along with the surge and withdrawal of steroids, hormones and pain medication, my emotions fluctuated wildly.

During the daytime, my sense of modesty and courtesy usually stifled my wishes to throttle the nurses who woke me up or accidentally yanked an IV. Sometimes the pounding in my head changed me into an uncouth bastard that had no patience for even the slightest inconveniences. The truth was, I could never predict when Mr. Hyde would emerge from beneath the bleached linen sheets of my hospital bed to snap some rude comment to whoever had pissed me off. My mental stability was at the whim of the chemicals that coursed through my body.

At night, I was quieter, but a tortured soul. Many, including my mother, might describe me as a night person – I always have been. Nighttime is when I'm at my most reflective. Mental acuity can focus in the absence of distractions like television, noise or other people. Lying in that hospital bed, my sadistic mind besieged me with thoughts of death, my funeral, cancerous cells roaming freely, and the look on my family's faces should I die. I spent hours upon hours trudging through the muck of these and related thoughts. I tried to remind myself to remain positive, to stay strong. But those doses of morphine wore off and I lay sweating and hurting in my bed, it was hard to be optimistic. As sure as I was that I would survive this ordeal, we all need to release the negativity that builds up behind the scenes. Darkness provided me a realm to release some of those fears.

During the hours that I lay awake in my bed, the night nurses would often come in to check my temperature and blood pressure. Every four hours, to be exact. They too developed characters in my melodrama. When I lay wide-eyed and terrified, they entered as quiet heroines. They came to distract me from the hell that unfolded in scenes upon the shadowy ceiling above my bed. Their cold glass thermometers and latex-pulse-taking-hands were more human than anything going on inside my head. However, as the night dragged on and they continued to barged through that door to wake me up to take my damn temperature every four hours, I feel like I could have killed them. (Well, if I could have gotten out of bed I would have killed them). They changed from heroines to villians all in the course of a single evening.

Gradually my body began to cooperate with my attempts to recuperate. Sleep arrived more frequently and eventually came as often as the awful thoughts. Of course, that meant that the nurses woke me up more than they saved me, but then, I was less murderous too. Days turned into nights of semi-restful sleep, which turned into days of semi-consciousness. As days turned into weeks, the complications began to level out and come under control.

Steroids continued to wreak havoc on the world, but for the first time in weeks, my fever had begun to fall. The physicians waited patiently for my blood counts (especially my white blood cell count) to rise to an acceptable level before I would be allowed to return home. I waited not-as-patiently. Meanwhile, my house was being cleaned and readied for my arrival. The walls were bleached, the rugs steam cleaned and everything wiped down. My blood was taken every morning and Dr. Schenkein informed me of the progress during his rounds.

Each morning he arrived with a trio of numbers. That happy little family of three numbers that described to me how my progress was coming. It was amazing the power that these numbers held over me. The red blood cell count told me how much energy I had. The platelet count told me if I needed a blood infusion. But that damn white blood cell count – well it wielded the power of my freedom. Each day it grew just a touch or dipped just a little. A thousand cells here, a thousand there. As long as they continued to go up, I knew that Jessica's marrow had successfully found a new home inside my bones and had started growing. If the counts dropped, it may have meant that her marrow had been rejected, or more dangerously, it had rejected me. Luckily those numbers kept growing. Two steps forward and one step back. 1500, 1650, 1600, 1900, 2100, 2000, 2400. But they just kept rising.

As soon as Dr. Schenkein felt they were high enough, I could leave this prison. There was a fortunate overlap between the periods of intense pain and the drug induced comas. As my strength slowly returned, I began to hate those four stark white walls that seemed to inch their way in each morning. As the morphine and Ativan slowly worked their way out of my system, I was left with just fatigue, dull pain, anxiety and those damn four walls. The platelets, red and white blood cells would multiply and multiply until they reached whatever number Dr. Schenkein needed. Until they hit that number, I waited.

I remained in the hospital for thirty one days. It turns out I had just missed the record for shortest stay by only one day. As a highly competitive person, that sucks. On August 20, 1996 I was sent home to begin the long process of recuperation. Unfortunately, home wouldn't prove to be much better than the hospital, but at least I was at home - carpeting on every floor!

But I was still playing the waiting game. And Jessica's bone marrow was in there sapping every ounce of my strength as it tried to fill the void left by chemotherapy.

Chapter 18

"Cousin's Marrow Gives Roderick A Chance, But He's Still Got A Long Fight Ahead"
 - Front-page headline of the Wareham Courier

My body was beginning to recover from the acute effects of the chemotherapy, but it still had much to do. I was too weak to get out of bed, and slept fifteen or sixteen hours a day because I was so exhausted. I didn't eat much because I was overwhelmingly nauseous. Everyone that came over wore a mask and latex gloves to protect me from infectious bacteria. I was taking forty pills a day, and couldn't sleep without medication. I was also in excruciating pain and took Demerol every few hours to quiet my screaming body. Medications continued to ravage my body. These drugs were designed to help me ward off infections, to prevent graft versus host disease, to boost my red and white blood cell count, to prevent nausea and a host of other medical reasons. Unfortunately, each medication comes with a side effect.

In fact, some of the drugs I had to take was to curb the effects of others. For example, the prednisone steroids continued to keep me awake each night so I needed sleeping pills. A drug designed to help bolster my immune system produced terrible pain in my spine, which required a strong painkiller. Many of the drugs made me queasy so the physicians prescribed an anti-nausea medication. Something caused massive cramps in my legs, which required heavy doses of magnesium. The constant intravenous Cyclosporine made my hands tremble wildly. This push-pull system of medicine requires careful balancing by both the physician and patient. I was careful not to allow each and every symptom to be treated with a drug if I could deal with it on my own. I attempted to use the painkillers and anti-nausea medication only when needed, but the fact remained that the cure was doing more to harm me now than the disease.

I faced a host of new and disturbing side effects as the chemical stew ebbed and flowed through my body. Some unknown mixture of substances robbed me of my entire short-term memory. I would struggle to stagger into a different room, and then forget why I had to go there. In retrospect, it is slightly humorous - it has to be. My hands and feet tingled once again with the familiar and annoying pins-and-needles I had experiences with earlier rounds of chemotherapy.

During the first few weeks, a nurse came every day to administer medications through my IV. The schedule was almost as regimented as in the hospital; only here I was able to use my own bathroom. Each morning a different nurse arrived to hang medications and clean the rubber hose dangling from my left chest. She would prepare her kit of gauze, iodine, tape, and cotton swabs. Then she would causally tear the old tape and gauze off my chest, poke and prod the hole with iodine, and redress it with artistic flare. All of this with a smile.

Most mornings it was nice to see a new face in the house, but sometimes – well, lady I'm just not in the mood for your joviality.

She would then check my pulse, measure my blood pressure, tap my belly and the rest of those superficial tests that rarely shed light on anything. *It's all on the inside!* I wanted to yell at her. We've waited by the phone for the MRI results, or the blood work to come back from the lab. We know that in most cases, these routine checks are more for formality and to rule out only the most obvious causes of illness. I was dealing with something she could not feel. I know it was her job but sometimes I was just angry and it felt too routine.

The new marrow was struggling to take hold deep within me. Cell by cell it clung to the inside of my bones and reproduced. I began with five percent of the stem cells I would need to produce enough blood cells to sustain me. Each day those cells multiplied. If my body didn't reject them as foreign, I would someday smell fresh air again. And here this silly lady is feeling my pulse and watching her second hand. I was dealing with months and years – she was concerned with her second hand.

Then there were the IV poles. At one point, I had two large ones. The twin towers. They made going to the bathroom down the hall a real pain in the ass. Eventually, as the meds were slowly reduced, I got to dump one of the poles. The other one continued to follow me around. It had lost its identical friend, but he still stood there, watching me. Day and night. The Cyclosporine had its own little pump about the size of a Walkman. That thing went with me everywhere – for weeks. Many drugs were taken away from the pole, but new ones took their places. As time went on, I could release it for a few hours, but it was always there.

It was almost a month before I was allowed to have visitors. My family was first to come visit. The grandmothers and aunts came by, a few cousins, but my mother was sure to restrict the number of visitors. Each person that walked through the door harbored the possibility of coughing or sneezing the germs that could prove fatally ill to her child. She was vigilant in her demands that each person to enter the house wear a mask and gloves. Friends and family continued to send cards, pray for me, and come to visit while I lay in my house fighting to recuperate.

Then an old friend began coming by every few days. Sibby Vespa was a girl with whom I'd gone to high school and worked with at a local pizza joint as well. She was even at the karaoke night before I entered New England Medical Center. She started coming once a week, then every few days, until she was coming every day. She visited just to keep me company, and it was amazingly helpful to my health. We put together jigsaw puzzles, we watched movies and we talked. She helped distract me from the array of plastic tubing, pump machines and dozens of pills I swallowed all day long. I finally had something to look forward to each evening as our relationship continued to grow stronger along with my health. Finally, something to get up for every morning besides the faces of some new nurse ready to hang the drug du jour.

At first, the nurses came every day. But ever so gradually, week by tedious week, they began to come less often. Don't get me wrong, I greatly appreciated the women (there were no men) who came every day to care for me. I valued their cheerful attempts to brighten my spirits and to refuel the IV's. However, my mother and I took pride in our ability to remain independent. I slowly learned how to hang the intravenous medications myself, how to connect the IV tubing, how to regulate the flow of these fluids. I even learned how to poke and prod at the hole in my chest all by myself. Soon we didn't need the nurse more than once a week or so. Week by week, day by day, hour by hour, I moved closer to "normal". Now those seconds the nurses counted off were making more sense to me. If I could take it one day at a time, I might make it through this yet.

But time passed slowly, and after each checkup, my oncologists informed me of the steady improvement in my blood count levels. "Leukocytes improving, great erythrocyte count, and oh my, look at those platelets!" My recovery until this point was nothing short of miraculous. There were no signs of major graft versus host disease and my blood counts were higher than expected. Bone marrow transplantation patients quickly learn that the first hundred days are the most critical because of the possibility of infection. I eventually passed that first milestone with few complications.

However, Dr. Schenkein warned me to be vigilant in my hygiene and precautions lest I still get an infection. For years we go through our daily lives unconcerned about the many activities that can lead to infection. I was brainwashed about the importance of avoiding germs to the point that it still permeates my daily life. During this period in my recovery, I washed my hands twenty to twenty-five times a day with antibacterial soap. I would not be in the presence of friends who were even remotely sick, and I actually got scared to be around someone who was sneezing. Even now, I wash my hands excessively and am paranoid about coming in contact with germs and bacteria. Touching doorknobs, shaking hands, or even blowing my own nose, I still feel that small twinge of paranoia. I know I'm being irrational, but I can't stop it. Over the years I've grown less neurotic but still harbor many of the same fears.

Dr. Schenkein informed me that my progress was so going so well in fact that I could start going outside. Soon people coming to visit would not need to wear the masks and gloves anymore. I was thankful for both accomplishments. I was sick and tired of being cooped up in my ever-shrinking house, and having everyone tip-toeing around me in a mask was something that I never seemed to get used to. I realized why I needed to take these precautions, but seeing my family and friends have to put on a mask to come near me was heart wrenching. It continued to remind me how far I was from "normal." They can't even come near me without that stuff on. I'm such a freak. Sometimes I wondered if the masks weren't more to protect them from my awful disease.

However, my good fortune was not completely without complications. I found myself back in New England Medical Center several times with fevers that suggested a possibly life-threatening infection. My mother and I were on constant guard for these fevers. If I sustained a temperature higher than 100 degrees for more than forty-eight hours, I needed to report to the hospital. I'd be forced to stay in the hospital, and on intravenous antibiotics, for a few days until the fever dissipated. No patient ever likes going back to the hospital. It felt like a step backwards.

About a month into the recovery, I began to have a terrible pain in my neck (no pun intended) and was getting dizzy. After several days of this, I told my mom who promptly carted me back to New England Medical to have it checked out. By that time, I was engaged in a complete "love-hate" relationship with the hospital, but something told me the pain was serious. It turned out I had a blood clot in my carotid artery that was disrupting the flow of blood to my head. I was readmitted to the hospital for three days and required to stay on Coumadin (an intravenous blood thinner) until the blood clot disappeared. If the blood clot had dislodged and found its way to my brain, I might have suffered a fatal stroke.

The most serious and most painful complication I encountered was shortly before Thanksgiving of 1996 - three months after I was released. My right arm began to hurt tremendously. It started off as short flashes of dull pain up my right forearm. In the backdrop of the many unexplained pains and aches of a bone marrow transplant patient, I was unworried. As the flashes came more frequently and gradually blended into one long ache, I took notice. As that ache grew to throbbing, I took action. None of the pain relievers I took seemed to lessen the agonizing pain, and all of a sudden, I began to notice small bumps and rashes on the skin of my arm. After a few test, Dr. Schenkein informed me that I had shingles. Shingles is a condition caused by the reactivation of chickenpox viruses, called varicella zoster virus or herpes zoster. Many bone marrow transplant patients develop shingles during the first year post-transplant. The virus settles around certain nerves resulting in inflammation, pain, and a rash of small skin blisters that usually extend along one of the body's nerve branches.

    The rash got much, much worse, and soon covered most of the arm from my fingers to my shoulder. Luckily for me, the virus was caught before it infected my spinal column, which can lead to unbelievable pain throughout the body, possible paralysis, and eventually death. My right arm is enough thanks. The rash looked like cold sores one might get on their mouth. Shingles is related to the virus that creates those as well. I cannot begin to explain the kind of pain this affliction produces. Since it is an infection of the actual nerve endings, no pain reliever, muscle relaxant, or medication would do a decent job of deadening the pain.

I have fractured my right arm, and shattered a knuckle in my right hand before. I am certain this pain was immensely greater than either of those. It didn't matter how tenderly I cradled my arm, whether I elevated or lowered it, moved it or didn't move it, the pain enveloped my entire day (and night) for the next two months. I could not sleep. I could not smile. I could not concentrate with this constant pain. It was not a sharp piercing pain, rather a dull thorough ache that cut straight through my muscles to the bone. Throughout my tenuous relationship with the healthcare community, I have faced a great deal of pain. Well-meaning physicians have alleviated much of it. Some of it has been cause by well-meaning physicians. I cannot explain in such vivid detail the extent to which shingles plied me with agony. Every morning, noon and night, I was haunted with this dull ache that disrupted my thoughts, my words and, most critically, my moods.

The shingles also sent me back to that institution of disinfectants and x-rays that I couldn't stand. On Thanksgiving Day, 1996, I was admitted to New England Medical Center. To add salt to the wound, I was also forced to eat the hospital's lousy attempt at a Thanksgiving dinner.

The following afternoon, my father brought up leftovers, but I'm afraid to say I didn't feel that I had much to be thankful for. I remained in the hospital for the better part of a week, where I continued to ask for drugs to keep me sedated as I dealt with the pain. When I was released, I was given another prescription for Demerol and was told the pain and rashes would slowly dissipate over the course of the following months. Acyclovir is prescribed to help fight the virus, but as with most viral infections, the patient just has to wait and heal. To this day, my arm remains itchy sometimes for no good reason, and there are some patches where my skin does not tan very well. It is not very noticeable, but serves as a visible reminder of one of this excruciating battle.

The relationship I had with Sibby continued to grow closer through all of these trials, until it became something much closer than friendship. Our connection was fused under the heat of a life and death situation where each day was a small miracle. She grew to love me, yet didn't know if I'd be alive the following month. I also was able to release my fears and allow my heart to grasp something human again. From a world of linoleum and fluorescent lights, I surfaced to the eyes of a beautiful woman who was willing to give me a chance. The pressure of our relationship forced us to form a bond artificially fast.

However, I also realized that she had a two-year-old son living with her at her apartment, and that our relationship was important to more than two people. Logically, I knew that it was a situation I should think long and hard about before jumping into. But I also knew I had feelings for this young woman, which I couldn't deny. Each day she arrived at my parents' house with a huge smile, and warm hug to wash down those forty pills. I knew her son was her world and I was willing to do anything to be with her. Sibby never asked me to be a surrogate father. Hell, I hadn't even been allowed to leave my house before our relationship began. But she did ask me to respect her situation, so I did. In return, she continued to stand by and support me as I recovered. Eventually we began to try to figure out how our relationship would change as I got to know and even became attached to her son.

Sibby showed me many things I would never have learned with my Ivy-League education. She was a constant source of inspiration and admiration as I saw how bent she was on providing her son with a good life. Admittedly, I was not much help in her endeavor, though I tried as hard as I could for a nineteen-year-old boy who was completely foreign to the situation. She helped me deal with the initial awkwardness and never asked that I do more than love her and respect her family. She was there to lean on as I continued to gain weight and get over the constant pain.

Unfortunately, the pain took an active role in almost all of my relationships. The most poignant of which was with my mother. Poor Ma. She took the brunt of my exasperation and resentment. Like the first soldiers on the beaches of Normandy, she was shelled each morning when she woke me. My rapid-fire grumbling and not-uncommon outbursts must have wreaked havoc on the poor woman. The anger was not usually directed at her, but centered on the pain and weakness I felt – she was just a convenient scapegoat. When my body would not react to my commands as they once had and as the painkillers wore off, I needed something, someone, to yell at. Most of the time it was my mom, sometimes it was Sibby. I hope she knew I never meant to hurt her. It was just an unconscious and immature way of coping.

Looking back, I saw firsthand how a primary caregiver must go through amazing pains to attend to their loved ones. My mother had already sacrificed a career for her children. She'd stayed at home to take care of us while my father earned the keep. She was our savior in the hospital setting. She knew what those doctors meant when they used the strange Latin words. But how tiring, how demanding it must have been to be at home with your cantankerous pain-in-the-ass son each and every day. Here she was, forfeiting her chance of a free life – and her first born is hurling abuse at her.

I found more strength to hide my frustration from Sibby though. Each day she continued to show up with those smiles and hugs – wearing that stupid mask and latex gloves. Okay, okay, so I wouldn't have seen her smile if she'd worn the mask the entire time. Rules were meant to be broken. My sentence at home was 90 days. I was unable to leave my house for 3 months straight. Sibby continued to show up and don the prescribed outfit just to see me. After a time, Dr. Schenkein informed me that my blood counts had improved enough to allow visitors to skip the precautions. What a glorious day! I was finally able to see Sibby's face sans mask and feel her hands without the odd latex gloves getting in the way.

Each day, each week my counts continued to improve. There were the expected setbacks such as the shingles and the blood clot, but overall my progress was steady. By steady, I do not mean quickly, but gradually. After about two months, I was given the green light to leave my house. Dr. Schenkein told me that I could go outside, but I was ordered to stay away from large groups of people. He even gave me a present. It was a silver bracelet that read, "Bone Marrow Trans/ Irradiated Blood/ Prod Only CMV Neg." Not very romantic, Doctor.

What that bracelet meant was no mall, no movies, and no restaurants. It meant that should I pass out or get into an accident, I had a bone marrow transplant, I would need irradiated blood (without viruses or bacteria) and it would need to be cytomegalovirus (CMV) negative. I could leave my house, but the immune system still wasn't ready for much. *I can't go to the mall or the movies or anything? What the hell will I do then?*

It turns out that for all my enthusiasm, I could barely walk to the end of the street and back. My erythrocyte (red blood cell) count was improving but still far from normal. I was anemic and didn't have enough oxygen to walk long distances without becoming immensely fatigued. I was still sleeping twelve hours a day as Jessica's marrow engrafted into my bones. So a trip to the mall was quite a moot point.

These new blood cells also had a sort of "boot camp" to go through. For nineteen years, my body had trained my lymphocytes. Each white blood cell travels through the thymus gland and is trained in how to recognize and fight foreign bodies. They are also equipped to "remember" those foes in case they should meet again.

However, these new cells had never been in my body before. They were all new to the game – not quite sure what they should do. It would take time for my body and Jessica's marrow to strike a peace accord and begin fighting the real bad guys – pneumonia, bacteria, whooping cough.

Once my white blood cell count was within the normal range, and Dr. Schenkein felt I was safe, I was able to go visit friends. Of course, with most of my friends off enjoying college, I only had one destination – Sibby's house. I began spending more and more time with Sibby and her son. The opportunity to escape solitary confinement was exhilarating and I spent as little time at home as possible. My mother persistently pleaded with me to "not overdo it", but I needed to get out. Sibby was again my breath of fresh air.

Our relationship and my marrow grew stronger – step by step. As weeks turned into months, Dr. Schenkein was pleased with my quick progress. The effects of the shingles diminished each day and soon the agonizing pain was reduced to a mere soreness. Don't misread me. This miraculous recovery was not simple. But as medications were reduced, so were my problems. The medicine that caused my back to ache stopped first – I was able to sit for longer periods. The steroids that made me agitated were dialed down – I was able to concentrate more. The medications that made me nauseous were decreased – I was able to eat more food and gain weight.

By the end of the fall, my eyes were set on my next goal. Returning to Dartmouth would be the apex of my achievement. I would not have simply survived; I would have arrived back at the place where my train had derailed. My life would be back on track. The mile-long train of iron that knocked me down would somehow pick me up and transport me back to where I belonged. If I could only get back to Dartmouth, this nightmare would be over – for now.

Sibby and I had an amazing time learning from each other, learning to love one another. She knew that my heart was also set on returning to school. We didn't know what that would do to us, but it was always there. We watched the colors of the leaves turn bright colors and fall from the trees. We then watched as the winter came. The snow covered the ground and turned everything cold. I was vigilant to monitor my health. No one was sure whether my immune system was yet ready to do battle with the flu or pneumonia. So I stayed bundled up as my body continued to grow. Each month the scale heralded me with five more pounds. White snow continued to cover the seeds of spring. My bones encapsulated a spongy marrow from which my new life would bloom.

A sudden love soon had to face a new future. As the winter came to a close, I was set to return to Dartmouth. As young lovers do, Sibby and I swore the distance would not separate us. Nothing could tear us apart – we were in love. Though try as we might, reality is stronger than fantasy. Our love turned into resentment when we couldn't be together physically. I wish I had the maturity to see what we were doing, but I didn't. Sibby and I fought when we spoke on the phone, and were both miserable. Our relationship ended halfway through my first term back at Dartmouth, and I was pretty heartbroken. I still think of her often and know that she served as an amazing supporter during my recovery. She was a reason to get up each morning and fight through the pain and fatigue to begin enjoying life again. Love is an amazing motivator.

Chapter 19

Live each day as you would climb a mountain. An occasional glance toward the summit keeps the goal in mind, but many beautiful scenes are to be observed from each new vantage point. So climb slowly, enjoying each passing moment; and then the view from the summit will serve a more rewarding climax for your journey.
- Bishop Fulton J. Sheen

Exactly one year to the day, I returned to the place upon which I'd set my sights - Dartmouth College. It took several months to get into the swing of academic life and even longer to navigate my way back into the social landscape. However, after a series of public blunders, mostly involving keg beer, I was sufficiently re-indoctrinated into college life. I'd returned from a horrific nightmare to resume the same life I had before I came out of remission. The only problem was that it wasn't the same life. It was a life made richer, more aware, and I wasn't the same person – I was forever changed.

It was strange and confusing trying to transition back to "normal." For years, normal was all I wanted to be. When I left halfway through my freshmen year, people were still getting to know each other, trying to figure out who they are and where they fit. As I lay in the hospital, that process was put on hold for me. Returning was made more difficult not only because I'd been away from the rigorous academia of an Ivy League college, but the social landscape had changed dramatically. I came back to find the various cliques and social circles that had already formed and all of my friends were entrenched in their routines and agendas.

Where do I fit in, where can my friends make the space and time for me in these agendas? Where do I want to fit?

At first I didn't fit in anywhere. My friends were overjoyed to have me back, but it would take time to figure out where my presence could be incorporated again. This was probably the hardest thing about returning. Dealing with the stresses of my academic pursuits was tackled in a fairly short time, but it was this social structure to which I had a hard time adapting. At times it was painful and depressing, but I was forced to remind myself it would take time for everything to work itself out. Besides, I certainly had been through worse. As I expected, it got better and I finally carved out a place for myself again. I was a decorated battle general now. The new suit of self-confidence, durability and perspective fit me well.

On the other hand, this desire to become normal again was increasingly confusing. For many months surrounding the transplant, my everyday routines were extraordinary and out of the realm of normal experiences. I'd spent almost a year fighting constant pain, restrictions, limitations in my physical capabilities, and emotions that, at many times, seemed impossible to overcome. Every day a new medical problem arose to be dealt with, and any semblance of a normal life was constantly challenged. Nights were spent imagining my funeral and contemplating what would happen if I died. "Normal" had taken on a different meaning.

All I had wanted was to be myself again, but I wasn't the same person anymore. Things were strange to me. I wasn't concerned about some of the things my friends were, and more anxious about others. The "right" clothes didn't matter, but a sleepless night did. After trying for months to "fit in," I wasn't sure I wanted to be normal anymore. I returned to college to see so many people I knew living their lives blindly. Each new flower that opened this spring was a small miracle to me. Each day was a blessing. It was hard to relate to my peers – they hadn't yet seen what I had.

Every day I adapted a little more. As humans, that's what we're designed to do. Our brains are simply organs that are designed to make decisions that affect our survival. Over the course of millions of years, protozoa turned into hairy little creatures, which turned into Albert Einstein and Martin Luther King. Just as our lungs allow us to breathe air, as our liver filters blood, our brains help us make decisions that affect our survival. Adaptation is the supreme achievement of this evolutionary endeavor. I was slowly adapting to life post-transplant – back in the realm of the normal. But somewhere, this little voice kept shouting at me.

Kyle, this test isn't that important – life is! Stop stressing - at least you're alive!

It felt like a new battle to fight. I lived in a world created by Volvo-driving baby boomers. The most important thing I could do was get a job and buy an expensive house. I was also at a school where many of my peers had trust funds and the latest SUV model. Yet, here I was, straight from the depths of chemo-induced hell with a completely different view of the world. I had no clue what normal was supposed to be anymore. I didn't feel bett

As spring rolled into summer, I was almost back to 100%. My body was feeling almost the same as it had prior to the transplant. Everything worked as it had before. My new immune system was a well-oiled-T-cell-producing machine. And I had a girls' blood. My body had taken on my cousin Jessica's marrow and blood without rejections. While this is slightly odd, it provides two important benefits. If, in fact, I truly had X-linked Lymphoproliferative Syndrome, I now had new X chromosomes. The immune deficiency that began this process should be long gone. The other fortunate consequence of having her blood is that whenever I am grumpy, I can make a case that it is related to PMS. It never works but I keep trying.

The summer also brought the first anniversary of my bone marrow transplant. With the weather changing, it began to stir emotions and feelings that I hadn't expected. I had somehow staved off such sentimentality until summer nostalgia made memories of the transplant more salient. Unexpectedly, I was overcome by sensations that revealed to me just how profoundly this experience had changed me. Indeed, it has changed the very foundations of my spirit and perceptions. I become aware of a new sense of myself that had not completely surfaced. It took time to swim through my fear of survival to see the blessing that this ordeal has afforded me. The confusion of trying to find a new normal slowly gave way to this new found sense of self. All year long it was there, just below the surface. Like a swimmer just underwater, its shadowy form sprang from my unconsciousness. As these new emotions arose, I noticed a tangible difference in my attitudes. I not only lost the resentment and anger, but I found myself steeped in positivity. I am happy to be alive today!

Being somewhat removed from the transplant my memory seems melodramatic. However, the undiminished fears and apprehensions give me an outlook that I never could have fathomed otherwise. My life is enriched in ways I never imagined. Thinking about pain, suffering, and death is extremely difficult for anyone to contemplate. At a tender age, I was forced to make life or death medical decisions. I faced my own mortality in a way that seemed both unfair and too early. However, now that I have survived this ordeal, my days are enriched by a love of life that I could not have understood under any other set of circumstances. This fascination with the mundane is now my reality, therefore I will let you decide for yourself whether my memory is melodramatic.

The key to this new gift is an awareness of the frailty of our lives. Fleeting moments are all we will really ever have aren't they? I recognize now that I can plan for the future, I can learn from the past, but all I really have is right now. A string of moments woven into a fabric that appears seamless. Once I had everything taken away from me, I could truly see each moment for what it was. Of course, I don't walk around in a stupor blinded by everything amazing and positive going on around me. But I have chosen to take this opportunity to become sensitized to the magnificence that we encounter every single day. I don't have the time nor the inclination to complain about the little things anymore, it's simply not worth the time or aggravation. Instead I try to focus on the positive, focus on the good.

I hear the beauty of spring birds singing of their awakening. I feel the glorious dark earth under my bare feet. I smell freshly cut green grass as the nitrogen swirls in my nostrils. I stare into the blazing reds, oranges, yellows, and purples of a sunset that no artist or television screen could reproduce. These are the things that truly matter, the experiences that give our lives meaning. Extending a hand first for a handshake. Showing gratitude. Saying sorry. Not being so uptight. Make the best of what is given. Know that if it all ended tomorrow, I should have absolutely no regrets.

My whole value system and sense of awareness has shifted so dramatically that the summer of the transplant has been nothing short of a rebirth. That's not to say that I'm glad I was forced to struggle through such difficult times in order to acquire this gift. It's a vantage point that came with much sacrifice and loss, but one that I have chosen to cherish to steal from the anguish.

I yearn to share this lesson with everyone I meet. I have an insatiable hunger to teach people what I know. That is the only way to make my pain serve another purpose, to make it worth all the suffering. If I can just change one person's life, then it will help me to understand the reasons it had to be this way. I've written these words for myself, for others who must make a similar journey, and for my friends.

I'll give you an example. Within the first weeks of the summer, I experienced what I can only explain as a revelation. It was a rainy but warm summer afternoon. The rain poured down to quench the budding summer perennials. College students crouched under their umbrellas and held their rain jackets closed. I suddenly became aware of how alive I felt. It just hit me – like something I had forgotten and suddenly remembered with shock. How grateful I was to be alive. I removed my hood and raised my face to the gray, wet sky. It was the very sky I was unable to enjoy just one year before, as I lay isolated in my lonely hospital room.

The rain soaked my hair, and I could feel it run down my forehead, my eyes and neck. It collected on my cheeks and slowly ran down the tender sides of my neck. It began to wet my collar, yet I was more content and at ease with each drop as though it was somehow washing away the pain. The water collected upon my chest. It watered me like the blossoming flowers. I could not think of a single place that I would rather have been, and I let the rain continue to rinse clean those aching memories and replace them with this new beautiful revelation. Walking slowly around my now saturated campus, the intensity of this epiphany continued to grow. The same drizzle that my peers huddled against and ran from, melted away my fears, cooled the pain. This water was my baptism. All the anger was forever washed away. The rain that collected on my cheeks replaced the tears that I wept when I lost my innocence. The droplets that dribbled down my chest traced the lines of the plastic tubes that had haunted me for so many months. This water from the sky ran down my neck and blessed the scars that will forever mark my transition.

For a year, my only goals were to survive and get back to college. Finally, there I was, I made it. I was so content to realize this new sense of "aliveness" that I got the chills. Do you ever get the chills from seeing something moving, awe-inspiring? I have since been blessed with this gift far more than I previously enjoyed. To be walking slowly in the rain on this warm summer day, to be outside and experience it, allowed me to feel a beauty we rarely have the chance to experience.

Dartmouth College in Hanover, NH in autumn is one of the most amazing sights in our beautiful country. People travel from all over to see the reds, yellows, oranges that the White Mountains serve up each October. Each morning as I walked to class, I tread on a carpet of organic artistry. Nature continued to serve up its own brand of healing. The days continued to fall like individual leaves from the grand oaks and maples that surrounded my college campus. September came and I was alive to celebrate my sister's thirteenth birthday. October came and I returned home to carve pumpkins with Dana and my mom. November came and we all had much to be thankful for.

As the harsh winter approached New England, I decided to seek refuge somewhere warmer. I chose to apply for the exchange program at the University of California at San Diego. In fact, I had filled out the application several months prior but told no one. I kept the secret from my mother and father and sprang it on them just as the fall was winding to a windy end. I saw no need for them to worry until I was sure that I was prepared to leave for San Diego.

For years, I'd been tethered to a life of doctors and hospitals. My overprotective mother kept a close eye on every move I made, never coat left unbuttoned. Since my lymphoma diagnosis at seventeen, I felt at once claustrophobic and apprehensive about being far away from the people who had cared for me and helped me fight the evil mutant leukocytes. Finally, it was time for me to get away. California would be both an escape from the eagle eyes that watched me and a challenge for the new self that had sprung forth. Go west young man. So I applied for the exchange program, told my parents after I was accepted, and boarded a plane for the other side of the country.

As expected, my time in California was absolutely amazing. Each morning, warm sun streamed through the blinds in my room. Soft horizontal rays fell across my face as I wiped the sleep from eyes. Birds chirped to welcome me back to the world of the conscious and the few delicate clouds that hung in the sky greeted me as I left the apartment. The new smells of eucalyptus trees wafted into my nostrils and lent me an air of refreshment. If not quite re-birth, it was refreshing my awareness. The feelings and subtle revelations that surfaced during that momentous rainstorm were reawakened. Each sun-filled day wrapped me in happiness as I walked to class. It was almost hedonistic, the way my senses indulged in the new smells and sounds of the place. It had taken so much for me to realize how precious these small blessings were. Yet, I believe this ability lies in all of us, it only needs to be realized. A car accident, a gunshot, a terrible disease. Why does it cost so much to see something that is already there?

I think that all of us come across spiritual places in our lifetimes. Some places put us at peace a force us to rethink things. Sometimes we're too busy to stop and recognize them, but in California, I was open to this place. The cliffs stand three hundred feet in the air, overlooking the vast blue Pacific Ocean. A few times a week I would saunter down to the cliffs from my apartment. From atop these cliffs, I let the cool salty breeze caress my face. As the sun began to set, I let the deep reds, purples, and oranges burn memories onto the back of my eyes. It reminded me to stop my petty thoughts – to stop and redirect them. All of the noise of that Volvo-driving baby boomer world faded away. All I heard were waves far below and wind whipping past my ears. As I stared out over the ocean, I couldn't help but think about things bigger than myself, think about things more permanent. That ocean seems so infinite. My life, my world is such a small drop in that ocean. It has been here since long before me and will continue until the end of time. At those cliffs, my problems seemed so miniscule that nothing could bother me. The underlying current of everything I thought revolved around gratitude and perspective. How lucky am I to be alive. How lucky we ALL are to be alive – just to be here! That's enough.

Today, I'm not near those cliffs anymore so it's hard to re-experience what I realized. My cell phone constantly rings. My career path doesn't seem as straight as it once was. Relationships take time and energy to maintain. Deadlines seem just around the corner. Bills keep coming in the mail. However, I think the point is to keep trying. If I just keep trying to picture that sunset in my head, feel those rain drops running down my face, feel how I felt one hundred days post-transplant… if I just keep trying to remember how blessed I am to be alive, if I just keep trying to remember that today is the day that really matters – then my life will always be beautiful. All the rest is just noise and that noise should not interfere with the symphony of my life.

As for my current health, every year I visit the hematologist to check my status. My blood counts have been within the normal ranges for years now. My body shows no sign of graft versus host disease, nor any signs of Lymphoma. For many years it just felt like the waiting game. Damn, I'm sick of that game. *Am I cured? Will it come back? How long do I have to wait until I'm sure?* Typically, cancer patients must achieve five years of disease free survival to consider calling their treatment a "cure." The longer a patient survives the better the chances that the treatment was successful and killed every malignant cell. I was obviously hopeful that everything would work out and I would never be faced with this again. I pray that the transplant will turn out to be the miracle that my family and I truly hope it is.

I'm happy to say that as of this writing, I'm exactly 11 days from my 20th cancer free anniversary! I cannot, however, go without saying that I still remain worried that the Lymphoma may return. I often wonder what will happen if it came back. No one speaks much of it anymore, and that is why I am scared. You see, as long as I remain scared, a recurrence cannot surprise me. Should I release my anxiety and erase these memories from my mind I would be too vulnerable to the devastation. So my vigilance remains strong. It is every cancer patient's worst nightmare to think that all the pain and suffering they've endured will prove futile if their disease recurs.

    I used to wake up in cold sweats after having horribly vivid nightmares of going to the doctor's office for a checkup, and hearing that the cancer returned. The nighttime silence allowed the rats in my brain to roam free again. Not many of my family or friends knew anything of my fears and worries because, frankly, I felt that they could have no way to understand. How could they help me deal with these crippling emotions? There is nothing I could say to them, no way to explain how intense and frequent my fears of recurrence were. On the positive side, I use that fear as a tool to shape my everyday life and stop taking things for granted. Therefore, I remain vigilant not just to scare myself, but because it enriches me.

    At a tender age my mortality was challenged and the physical and psychological pain I've endured cannot truly be summed up within these few pages I've written. I certainly could have lost faith in my own strength or courage and succumbed to the many challenges that this disease has shown me. Instead, I remained determined to survive. From the moment I made the decision to risk my life in the hopes of a "cure", I had faith in myself. I was determined not simply to survive, but to persevere and live my life during whatever time I will eventually be granted on this earth. I have chosen to use all these horrifying experiences, and turned them into a unique gift. It's a gift I could only possess by seeing the end of my life. As I walk and breathe, I find a beauty in my life that was missing before this precious, invaluable gift.

With this gift, I learned to live my life to the fullest each and every day. So simple, right? No, we know it's not that easy. Those phone calls keep coming, that career path is still there, those relationships still need work and I still desire more money. But as I remember that vast ocean, I realize, that's just small stuff. If I focus on the bigger things, that small stuff will fall into place. When I take a step back, I realize things aren't always as important as they seem, it's just we seem so close to them. They are problems I'm creating in my own mind, problems I allowed myself to have.

I can see now that the people in my life are what I should care about - my sister, my parents, family and friends, people who need my help. They are what are truly important. Honesty, integrity, loving, understanding, observation, these are some of the things I cherish. I try to make it a priority in my life to let those people know how I feel about them deep down. We never know what will happen. So if I am open with my heart, perhaps it will rub off on them.

They have not been where I have been and I'm sure they will need to go through their own battles before they see the truth. I have been gifted enough to see the sun set over the Pacific ocean from atop those cliffs. The colors - red, pink, purple, orange, and yellow. I can compare my small problems to the IV poles, the weakness, and the thoughts of my funeral – then they don't seem as big anymore. We all relate things to our own experiences. That's how we rationalize things. But I'm hoping that if I keep trying to share my gift it will spread. I hope that someone, anyone, will see the pain I've gone through, and learn from it. That will make my survival worthwhile.

The biggest lesson I've learned was a promise I made to myself while lying in that bed in New England Medical Center.

Okay Kyle, if you make it through this, you can never look at things the same way. I know you took things for granted. I know you didn't always say what you should have. I know you said many things you shouldn't have. You should always be honest; because if you check out now there will be things that you should have fixed. But look, just make it out of this and I promise that I'll never live another day with any regrets. Let's just get out of this mess . . .

I still remember that promise and it fuels my desire to slow down, to talk to people, to see the miraculous beauty I'm surrounded with during the most ordinary days. It reminds me to live life to the fullest - without regrets. Cancer has shown me more pain than most people should know in their entire lifetime, but it has also shown me how I want to spend the rest of my time here - however long that may be. If adversity introduces you to yourself, then I find it fortunate that I like who I met. As an autobiography of a man who is still alive, it would be impossible to write the ending, but I promise when it is written – it will be a good one.

Dedication

This book is dedicated to the friends, family, and other loved ones who have helped me to scale mountainous obstacles. I truly believe that without your compassion, strength and continued prayers I may have never made it. I'm eternally grateful for your help and live a life enriched by your kindness and magnificence.

I originally started this manuscript as a form of self-therapy. I wrote this as a very young man and have decided to leave it in that voice. Professors and family tried to persuade me to publish it for years, but I was reluctant to let it go. I was apprehensive about exposing my story to others for fear it might dilute a vigilant concern I hold over my own health. As a cancer survivor, I'm terrified of the prospect of fighting a new battle. If I published this story as a static piece, I feared that fate may judge me brazen and presumptuous. This war might not be over and I'm not confident I have the energy left for another surprise attack.

In spite of successfully holding out after much pressure, my mother exposed the story anyway. Shortly after finishing the original manuscript, my mother wrapped her meddling hands around it. She shared this story with cancer survivors and caretakers throughout our small community. Folks soon approached me with tears in their eyes, the most memorable of whom was our neighbor, Pat.

Arriving at my parent's house early one evening, I wearily stepped from my car after driving home from Dartmouth. I'd arrived home for the holidays, after a several hours on the highway. As I began to unload dirty laundry from my trunk, a voice called to me, "Kyle, Kyle, can I talk to you?" my neighbor said as she ran across the street from her house. As she approached, I caught glimpse of emotion welling up in her brown eyes. "Hi, Miss Pat, what's going on?" I said with obvious trepidation. She explained that my mother had lent her a copy of my autobiography – after which I released an annoyed groan.

Pat continued to explain how much the story had touched her. Unbeknownst to me, she'd just finished treatment for breast cancer. "Kyle, you don't know how much your book has meant to me," she elaborated as tear rolled steadily down her cheeks. "It offered the first moments of hope I'd felt in months. To read about how someone else has gone through the same feelings and survived has given me new strength." She went on to say that it had been nearly impossible to explain how she'd felt to her own husband. The feelings of isolation, fear, anger, and bewilderment were difficult to express adequately to the man she loved. Pat highlighted each passage of my personal story that struck a chord with hers. She gave it to her husband and asked him to read it – paying particular attention to the highlights. When he finished they had a new understanding of each other. She continued to cry and held me for some time.

As Pat turned to walk home, her husband Bill emerged from the screen door. As I continued unpacking my car, I felt a heavy hand on my shoulder. Without words, Bill hugged me. "I just wanted to come over and thank you for writing those words," he said with eyes soaked in sincerity. "I never knew how she felt, Kyle. Thank you." He also cried and in an instant I knew they shared the same emotional soup I'd experienced – was continuing to experience. It was at that moment that I decided these few words I'd written for myself might be able to help other survivors and their loved ones.

Postscript

After surviving the bone marrow transplant in 1996 and several complications thereafter, I went on to graduate Dartmouth College. Within a few years, I was taken off medication completely and gradually became healthier and more vibrant than ever before. In 2013, I was blessed with the miracle of a baby boy. He is healthy, charming and handsome. His mother and I are immensely proud of his empathy and his determination. I hope I will play a small role in fostering those traits due to my illnesses and I'm allowed to live long into his life and watch him grow into a special man.

To my boy: You bring me more intense joy than I ever thought my heart could experience. When I found out we would welcome you into this world, I was overjoyed. Now that you're becoming your own person, I can't find the words to describe my feelings for you. I realize now why God spared me. He left me to help raise you. He left me so I could meet you. I'm grateful every day for this and I love you with all my heart.

Made in the USA
Las Vegas, NV
06 June 2021